HIDDEN IN BERLIN

A HOLOCAUST MEMOIR

EVELYN JOSEPH GROSSMAN

ISBN: 9789493056800 (ebook)
ISBN: 9789493056794 (paperback)
ISBN: 9789493231108 (hardcover)

Cover: Part of Wedding Photo - Elisabeth and Ernst Joseph, March 29, 1947

Copyright © 2020 Evelyn Joseph Grossman

Publisher: Amsterdam Publishers

info@amsterdampublishers.com

Holocaust Survivor True Stories WWII Book 6

For my grandchildren, Josie, Knox, and James

CONTENTS

ADVANCE PRAISE

"In this story Evelyn Grossman writes a very readable, thoroughly researched and emotionally gripping account of the experience of her parents and their families from 1932 until after the war. Some were taken from their homes in Berlin to be murdered. Others survived, hidden by angel Germans who risked their lives. As I read I knew what it was like to live every day always terribly afraid that I too would be caught and taken away to die. Be prepared. You will be unable to put this book down until you've finished it."

Rabbi Robert Freedman, ordained as both a cantor and a rabbi, has served congregations in Princeton, NJ, Manchester, VT and Philadelphia, PA.

* * *

"Behind the simple title lies a complex, multigenerational story set in Nazi Germany and in the United States. At the center are Lilo and Ernst, the author's parents. Through grit, courage and luck, aided by people from all walks of life, they, and Ernst's mother, Betty, survived. It is a story of love and determination and a story of heartbreaking loss and breathtaking miracles. It is a story of an unending search to discover the fate of those who did not survive and those who faded into the background after the war. It is a story about gratitude and rebirth - where the past lives in the present and the present in the past.

The narrative is interwoven with connections and trains of thought, which lead the reader from specific events to the larger context in which they occur. When in September 1942, Lilo and her brother, Hans Martin find the door to the family apartment sealed and their parents in Gestapo custody, the narrative pivots to the Wannsee Conference, Eichmann's role in it, and then to Lilo's reactions as she is glued to the TV in her apartment in New Jersey watching the Trial in Jerusalem in 1966. Similarly, when Lilo receives a letter from her half sister who was protected because of her "Mischling" status, the reader is lead to a reflection of what it means to be a Jew and from there to the Rosenstrasse Protest in 1943. And Lilo's first encounter with a portrait of Theodore Herzl leads to a discussion of Zionism and from there to Joachim Prinz, a courageous Rabbi in Berlin who emigrated to the US and spoke at the MLK March in 1963. Questions about religion, race, cultural identity and shared history are raised in the context of the Nazi laws about Mischlings.

The zigzag of the narrative, the extended time frame from Nazi Germany to contemporary America, and the inclusion of several generations provide a rich and unique perspective on a tragic historical period."

Dr. Eva Gossman, retired Associate Dean of the College, Princeton University and author of *Good Beyond Evil.*

1

LETTERS AND PHOTOS

I'm writing you this letter, but I don't know if you will receive it. I hope so . . . A long time has passed since we saw each other. More than 16 years. The time here for us has passed very quickly, too quickly . . . Forgive me my long silence . . . let us be old friends again, as we were before. You have no idea how happy that would make me. If there is something you want that I can help with, please let me know.

My father wrote those words in November 1964 to Oscar Materne, a good friend in Germany during the war years. A few weeks later, his widow replied. Her husband had died months ago. She was living quite modestly on a pension, and would welcome a small food package.

I remember sitting at the kitchen table in our house in Ewing Township, New Jersey, a suburb of Trenton, watching my father as he wrote letters on the clunky, old, black manual typewriter and filled cardboard boxes with cooking oil, coffee, tea, sugar, cocoa, and cigarettes. I was a teenager, old enough to know the outline of how my father had survived the Holocaust, but very few details.

Oscar Materne had been the connector. He was the one who found a German couple willing to shelter my father and grandparents. For 27 months, they hid in a small room in the center of Berlin. That much I knew from conversations in the house, but very little else.

There was never a time when I learned about the Holocaust. The past always had a place in our house, and bits of the story came out sporadically.

My father and mother grew up in pre-war Berlin, in Jewish homes with a strong German identity. Both families were registered by the government as part of the *Jüdische Gemeinde*, the Jewish Community, as were all Jews, regardless of any connection to a synagogue. The Joseph family, my father's side, celebrated Passover and Chanukah, but their cultural identity rested on their love of the German writers, Goethe and Schiller, and Austrian composers, Haydn and Schubert. The Jacoby family, my mother's side, came to the synagogue on Rosh Hashanah and Yom Kippur, and rarely, if at all, the rest of the year. Bruno Jacoby, my maternal grandfather, served with distinction during the Great War, a past he held on to with pride and, in his opinion, one that confirmed his loyalty to Germany.

My father's story and my mother's intersected at times, but for the most part, they remained distinct until their marriage after the war. My mother spoke of a childhood filled with dance classes, biking with her brother, and swimming in a public pool with artificial waves. She dreamed of becoming a ballerina. In those years during the Weimar Republic, there was no antisemitism. At least, that was the way she remembered it.

Perhaps there was no overt persecution in Charlottenburg, a progressive and upscale area in the western section of Berlin where the Jacoby family lived. Nonetheless, antisemitism was pervasive in Germany in the 1920s, with harassment in the universities, discrimination at work, and attacks on Jews in newspapers, flyers, and posters.

When the Gestapo came and marched my maternal grandparents away, it no longer mattered that Bruno Jacoby had been awarded the Iron Cross, first class.

My father was eight years older than my mother, a difference great enough that he was able to complete one year at the university, while my mother had to leave school at the age of fourteen.

When the Nazis closed the door of education, my father began working in the Central Market Hall with my grandfather. Leopold Joseph, my paternal grandfather, owned a business importing canned fish and selling to local merchants in Berlin. It was in the marketplace where my father met Oscar Materne.

I grew up in the 1950s, in a home with deep love and shadows of earlier days filled with pain. I am the daughter of German-Jewish parents who wanted to assimilate into their new country, even if they couldn't lose their accents.

An oil painting of Leopold Joseph hung over the fireplace mantel in our living room. My father rarely spoke of his father, but I believe he wanted that portrait to have a prominent place in our home as a sign of respect and a reminder that his father died while in hiding, three months before the war ended.

My mother has no photo of her mother, one of her father, and a few of her brother. That she had managed to save any photos is remarkable. My mother was the only one of her family who survived, and while she spoke often about them, mostly about her brother, the photos remained hidden in a shoebox in the closet.

In 1972, while I was in college, my father passed away suddenly from a heart attack. He lived a life of frugality and denied himself any luxury, determined to make a better life for his family. He succeeded, but at a cost of happiness. I know that he loved me deeply; and it's terribly hard to write these words without wiping my eyes.

I had not asked many questions about his experience during the war, as I was preoccupied with finishing school and beginning my own life. Over the next two decades, I was busy with a husband, two children, a job in finance, and a home in Princeton Junction, New Jersey. I still had not found time to learn the details of how my parents lived before and during the war.

In 1995, my mother and I traveled to Germany on a trip sponsored by the Berlin Senate. The trip was part of a program that invited Jewish residents who had fled Nazi Germany to return for a visit.

We toured Berlin, and I had the opportunity to thank Eva Cassirer, the woman who had saved my mother's life. The trip had a powerful impact on me—seeing the house that sheltered my mother during the war, walking the streets where my parents lived, and of course, meeting Eva. I resolved to write my mother's story and preserve her wartime experience. However, my kids, Eric and Amy, were then in high school, and I was working as a commercial real estate analyst at United Jersey Bank, and despite good intentions, my writing plans were put aside.

In 2008, the financial world collapsed, and I found myself unemployed. Eric and Amy had finished college, my husband, a physician with the Princeton Medical Group, was still working, and I decided to use this time to fulfill a promise made in Berlin.

The first thing I did was enroll in a German language class at Mercer County Community College. I already understood simple German, "kitchen German," but I needed to learn grammar, how to conjugate verbs in past and present tense, and formulate sentences with words in the right place. I wanted to read and review old letters and documents and engage in conversation in German. Classes at the community college led to more classes at Rutgers University and online courses with a German teacher, who became a friend.

The background for this memoir came from my father's written notes and a collection of his saved letters, along with notes from Uncle Gerhard, my father's brother, who immigrated to the United States before the war, plus my observations from trips to Germany.

By far, the largest component came from conversations with my mother. For years, we sat together on Sunday afternoons in her kitchen going through the box of old photos and letters, and while the tape recorder ran, we talked about the past.

I have written this story as a multi-generational memoir that unfolded in reaction to historical times, the destruction of Jewish life in Germany, and the catastrophic events of World War II. The narrative moves back and forth in time, with the intent of adding my perspective to my parents' story. The dialogue came through tape recordings, remembered conversations, and my understanding of how events occurred in time.

My parents lived in hiding in the center of Berlin. They survived years of antisemitism and persecution through their strength, the courage of a few extraordinary people, and a bit of luck that held the pieces together.

2

SEEKING SHELTER

Every day he heard more rumors. Every few days another train left for the east. Friends and neighbors disappeared, never any advance notice, simply a knock on the door. It was January 1943, and for more than a year, the Nazis had been deporting Jews from Berlin to labor camps. "Resettlement" to the east was the official explanation. No one had come back.

Ernst Joseph knew time was running out. He needed to find a hiding place, not just for himself, but a safe location for his parents as well. Alone, he could live on the street, in basements or bombed-out buildings, but not his parents, especially his father who had already suffered a heart attack. Finding a place for one person to hide was a challenge; finding a place for three would be a miracle.

Ernst was 27, slender, with a fair complexion, thin lips, and a rather narrow nose. His eyes were bright blue, and his dark-blond fine hair was already showing signs of a receding hairline. Except for the yellow-cloth star sewn neatly on his winter overcoat with "Jude" written in bold black lettering, he could have easily passed as a typical German, an Aryan.

In the early morning hour, with the sun barely visible and not providing any warmth, Ernst walked briskly to the train station to catch the S-Bahn. He walked with purpose, to arrive at his job at the Siemens factory[1] in the outskirts of the city on time. His mind was preoccupied, not by work but with a phone conversation he had had with Oscar Materne.

Materne was a business friend, a German, an outgoing, sociable man with a large network of connections, including Jewish merchants. He was a mature man, somewhere in his mid-fifties. He was certainly not a Nazi, yet he knew to be discreet about his political views. Ernst had grown to trust Materne and had spoken about his search for a hiding place. Materne had called the previous night. He had important information and wanted to see Ernst.

Ernst entered the train station, walked down the platform, and stood apart from the others. He glanced at his wristwatch, relieved to see there was ample time. He checked his yellow star to be sure it was visible and not covered by his woolen scarf. Such an act of carelessness could lead to questioning and even arrest. Ernst scanned the small group waiting for the train and caught sight of the police officer on patrol. He was a familiar fellow; the new ones could be difficult.

Ernst thought back on the conversation a few weeks earlier when this officer approached him and demanded to see his train card. Ernst handed him a ragged, pale orange card, his *Polizeiliche Erlaubnis*, his police permission card. The card, frayed around the edges from constant handling, was stamped with the

Nazi symbol, an eagle perched on top of a swastika. The officer examined the card, then sharply asked, "What's your name?"

"Ernst Joseph."

"What's your name?" the officer asked again, louder and harsher.

Ernst hesitated a moment and then replied, "Ernst Israel Joseph."

Since 1939, the government had required that the name Israel be added to the names of Jewish men and Sara to the names of Jewish women. In that same year the Nazis forced Jews to wear the yellow star, a mark of segregation and humiliation.

The officer continued, "Where do you live?"

"Kaiser Wilhelmstrasse, number 25."

"Rather close by." The officer frowned. "We make it easy for you to reach the station. So, where are you going?"

As the officer continued with his questions, Ernst heard the rumbling of an approaching train, the loud clamor of brakes bringing the train to a full stop, and the rustle of coats headed toward the open doors. Clearly, the officer had no intention of allowing him to leave, not now, not until he was finished with his questions. Ernst stood stiffly, worried not just by the delay but by where these questions were leading and what exactly the officer's intentions were.

"I work at the Siemens-Schukert factory, an hour train ride from here," Ernst replied.

The officer silently examined the card and returned it, saying, "I've wasted enough time with you." He looked directly at Ernst, then quickly turned around and walked away.

This morning, that officer who once questioned him, said nothing. Ernst walked down the platform, relieved to see a train approaching.

The ride to Siemens allowed him time to think about the upcoming meeting with Materne. He told himself to remain calm, to keep expectations under control. For so long Ernst had been talking to friends, Germans who were not Nazis. They understood the situation and empathized, but no one was willing to help. Hiding three Jews was too great a risk.

Ernst met Materne in 1938 when he began working at his father's business, Firma Lippmann, in the Central Market Hall in Berlin. Ernst had never intended to work in the market. He wanted to study astronomy at the university and for a short time, he did. As a boy, he spent hours adjusting the focus on his telescope, learning to spot the ragged W-shaped constellation of Cassiopeia and identify the bright light reflected from Venus. After completing his Abitur, the qualifying exam for university entrance, Ernst enrolled in Berlin University in 1933, following in the footsteps of his older brother, Gerhard. That was the year that Adolf Hitler was appointed chancellor.

It was a time of high unemployment and hyperinflation, and Hitler's message to disheartened Germans was clear: *Jews and Communists are to blame. Throw them out, your lives will be better.* Soon after the Nazis took control, new laws came into force, laws that severely limited Jewish enrollment. After his first year at the university, Ernst had to leave.

Gerhard, who had already completed his undergraduate work and was starting his doctoral thesis, was allowed to stay. His research focused on the effect of currency devaluation on the price of goods and services, a timely topic in the aftermath of the rapid inflation of the 1920s. While he found a professor willing to sponsor him, it was an uneasy time for the handful of remaining Jewish students. Many professors were Nazis who started and ended each lecture with "Heil Hitler." For those classes, Gerhard arrived late and left early.

After earning his doctorate degree in economics and law in 1937, Gerhard continued with postdoctoral research at the University of Basel.[2] Ernst had also made his way to Switzerland and for one semester both boys were safely out of Germany. At that time, Gerhard was thinking about leaving Germany for good. The first thing he needed was a passport, but requests from Jews were often delayed and sometimes denied, unless there was a good reason to travel. What if he had to travel to America for research? What if he needed specific documents available only in the libraries in New York City? That was exactly what one of his professors wrote and by the end of 1937, Gerhard had his passport.

In the spring of 1938, while Gerhard and Ernst were in Switzerland, a telegram arrived. Their father had suffered a heart attack. The boys returned home.

I imagine this telegram led to an extremely difficult conversation between my father and uncle. I will never know what was said, but the final outcome was that Gerhard left for America and my father stayed in Berlin. My father had always wanted to return to school and complete his education, and he believed his time would come, but not now. My father was 22 years old, and he viewed the world with the optimism of a young man, where in time, all things were possible.

On May 26, 1938, Uncle Gerhard boarded the passenger ship *Europa*[3] and departed for New York City. He traveled with a visitor's visa that only allowed a brief stay in America. He carried a list of names and addresses of people to contact, people who might be willing to sign an affidavit of support. With an affidavit, he would be able to stay in America. Otherwise, he would need to return to Germany.

As for my father, he soon became familiar with the winding rows of tables and merchants selling fruits, vegetables, meats, dairy products, and all sorts of canned goods in the Central Market Hall, an enclosed building of about 170,000 square feet. The market stood across the street from Alexanderplatz, a large public square, a popular center for shopping and for meeting friends. It was where people stopped for coffee, cake, and conversation and exchanged gossip, the best source of information.

Firma Lippmann, at stand 186, imported canned fish, such as sardines, herring, and mackerel from merchants throughout Europe. It was a wholesale operation that sold to small stores throughout Berlin. After his father's heart attack, Ernst took on the day-to-day responsibilities of unloading crates of canned fish, ordering merchandise from suppliers in Portugal, the Netherlands, and Spain, and soliciting orders from local retail shops.

The business was registered under the family surname, Lippmann. Yet Joseph was also the family name. These two last names caused endless confusion. At some unknown moment in the past, a mistake had happened, perhaps a typo or bureaucratic mix-up, and Leopold's middle name, Joseph, became his last name. Ernst grew up with various renditions of his name; sometimes he was called Ernst Lippmann, other times he was Ernst Joseph and, occasionally, Ernst Joseph-Lippmann. Not until he came to America after the war did the Lippmann name disappear.

My grandfather had succeeded in creating a business that provided a middle-class home for my grandmother, Berta (known as Betty to family and friends), and my father and uncle. A nanny had helped care for the boys when they were young, and there were a few summer trips to the Baltic Sea.

Ernst (back row) and Gerhard with their parents at the Baltic Sea

I imagine this undated photo of my father, Uncle Gerhard, and my grandparents on the beach was taken around 1926. I look at it often, and it breaks my heart to think about their future, a future they could never have imagined.

My father was born on July 15, 1915, and in the photo, I see a boy sitting in the back row, looking completely happy. I hardly recognize that boy as my father. I knew my father as a serious man and a protective parent, not someone who spent an afternoon at the beach. Yet in this photo, I see a smiling, carefree young boy.

Uncle Gerhard was born on April 18, 1914, and although he's only slightly older than my father, he already has the look of an adolescent. Perhaps his mind is elsewhere or he's just impatient for the photographer to finish. My grandparents are very properly dressed, especially my grandfather. With suspenders, tie, long-sleeved shirt, leather shoes, and newspaper in hand, he seems ready for a day at work. My grandmother is a bit more casual. She is resting her arm on my father's shoulder, and holding a shovel in her other hand, ready to dig sand tunnels. Seeing her in a dress does not surprise me. Oma lived with us for a few years when I was in elementary school, and I cannot remember a single day when she didn't wear a dress, stockings, and sensible shoes.

The year 1938, when Gerhard left for America and my father began working in the market, was a time of change, politically and domestically. Hitler's plans for territorial expansion became clear when Germany annexed Austria in March. Next, Hitler set his sights on Czechoslovakia. It had been just 20 years since the end of the Great War, and memories of loved ones lost still lingered. The Europeans did not want to engage in another war, and they accepted Hitler's words, his empty promises, and his lies. European leaders granted Germany possession of the Sudetenland, the western region of Czechoslovakia that borders Germany, in exchange for Hitler's promise not to seek further expansion. Prime Minister Neville Chamberlain of Great Britain signed the Munich Agreement, believing he had achieved "peace for our time."

Discrimination and persecution escalated in Germany, with restaurants, parks, and swimming pools banning Jews. The Nazis spread propaganda, labeling Jews as *Untermenschen*, subhumans, and storm troopers posted signs on Jewish stores that said, "*Kauft nicht bei Juden*," Don't buy from Jews.

On Wednesday night, November 9, 1938, flames erupted in cities throughout Germany. Nazi mobs marched into synagogues, ripped apart prayer books, tossed Torah scrolls on the street, and set synagogues on fire. Stormtroopers threw bricks into display windows of Jewish-owned stores, leaving broken glass, merchandise, and mannequins scattered everywhere. The S.A., the Brownshirts, broke into homes, arresting men and taking them to prison.

For two nights, the air was filled with men cursing and laughing, making sport of smashing windows. Fire trucks raced down the streets of Berlin with orders to protect German property, but not Jewish homes or burning synagogues.

After the second day there was silence. No alarms, just a handful of people making their way around broken glass. Fashionable hats lay torn and dirty on the street and hundreds of decorative buttons were covered by layers of glass splinters. But there was no merchandise in front of the jewelry stores, just shattered glass shelves and piles of opened boxes and dozens of empty trays.

This was *Kristallnacht*, the Night of Broken Glass, when the Nazis arrested 30,000 men, destroyed 7,000 stores, and burnt 250 synagogues.

My father and grandfather were arrested and taken to prison on Kristallnacht. I didn't know this until many years after my father died. I only learned about this part of my father's life from reading Gerhard's notes. After my uncle died in 1989, his daughter Judi gave me a copy of his writing. Gerhard had composed a brief history of his education in Berlin and the challenge of immigrating to America and finding a sponsor. In his notes he wrote about receiving a phone call from his mother in November 1938. She had terrible news: his father and brother had been arrested and were being held for ransom, 250 English pounds. This was a fortune for a young man who had come to America just a few months ago. To raise the money, Gerhard sold his Leica camera, borrowed money from friends and the Hebrew Free Loan Society.[4]

My father never talked about that night with me or my mother. I am left with sorrow for his pain, and I wonder how many other stories I never heard.

The pogrom of November 9 and 10, 1938, followed the murder of Ernst vom Rath, a German diplomat stationed in Paris. Herschel Grynszpan, a 17-year-old Jewish boy living with his aunt and uncle in Paris shot and killed Vom Rath. Grynszpan acted out of deep anger and a desire to avenge his parents, who had been forced by the Nazis, along with thousands of other Polish Jews, to leave Germany. Grynszpan's parents, who had been living in Germany for decades, were ordered to return to their native Poland. But Poland refused to allow them to enter, and they became stranded in refugee camps between two countries that didn't want them.

Propaganda minister Joseph Goebbels called the pogrom a spontaneous attack on Jews, their homes and synagogues, sparked by Vom Rath's killing. Yet years later, documents revealed that the attacks were far from spontaneous. Goebbels, the master manipulator, had planned this event months in advance.

Immediately after Kristallnacht, the Nazis forced Jews to sell their businesses at a government-determined selling price, far below market value. Proceeds from the sale were to be deposited in specified banks, from which only a limited amount could be withdrawn every month. Leopold complied with the orders but deposited only some of the proceeds in this type of blocked account. He kept most of the money hidden in the house.

Life in Berlin became increasingly oppressive. The Nazis ordered Leopold, a man in his sixties with heart problems, to work as a janitor and Ernst to take road construction jobs. In April 1941, Ernst began working *Zwangsarbeit*, forced labor, at Siemens. The Nazis brought Jewish men and women into the factories to replace workers drafted into the army and, above all, to maintain war production. Siemens paid Jewish workers very low wages, closely monitored their work, and sold the finished products to the government for military use, a profitable arrangement for Siemens. Ernst insulated cables used in submarines, and for a while, working at Siemens offered protection as he, along with other Jewish workers, supported the war efforts. The government needed their labor, and they were not deported. But no longer. The situation for Jews remaining in Nazi Germany was rapidly deteriorating.

Ernst arrived at Siemens on time and took his seat with the other men on a long wooden bench. Nazi guards and Siemens supervisors walked around the room. Ernst worked carefully, but in the back of his mind he thought about his recent conversation with Materne. He checked his watch constantly, impatient to leave for the day. He had kept in contact with Materne, often going over to the Central Market Hall after his father had sold the business. But tonight Materne wanted to meet elsewhere. A public place was fine, but not where everyone knew them. The men planned to meet by the clock at the Bahnhof Zoo railway station.

"Hey, Ernst, over here." Materne had arrived a bit early and stood waiting. "Ernst, you look terrible. Why do you always look so sad? That's not good."

"So, do you have any news?" Ernst asked, knowing Materne could go on and on. He was anxious, knowing so many earlier ideas had led nowhere.

Materne paused, glanced over his shoulder before replying, "Let's walk a bit."

Bahnhof Zoo, one of the busiest spots in Berlin, was the central train station for the S-Bahn and U-Bahn lines and a popular meeting place for teenagers. Not wanting to be overheard, Materne waited until they had walked past the entrance doors of the station. "Ernst, I have tremendous news. I found somebody who can help you and your parents."[5]

Ernst nodded, listened in silence, waiting to hear more.

"They're a couple, a husband and wife. I know the man, a good man, but I don't know the wife. He tells me she's just as strongly anti-Nazi as he is. Anyway, they've agreed to hide you."

Ernst looked around quickly. Nobody was standing close by. Nobody was listening. He took a few deep breaths, stared at Materne, and whispered, "Who are these people?" As excited as he was, his immediate reaction was caution. "Materne, can we trust them?"

"I trust them; why else would I be here talking to you?" Materne replied. "He works in the market, delivers merchandise. Ernst, you worry too much. You want to plan everything out, but there's no time now." Materne handed Ernst a slip of paper. "Here's his name and address. I've arranged for you to meet tomorrow evening. Now go home and be confident."

Ernst's head was spinning with indecision, with jubilation giving way to sharp jabs of panic. Who was this man? Could he be trusted or was it a trap? And what about the wife? If they were informers for the Gestapo, the secret state police, meeting them would result in deportation. *Am I bringing my parents into danger? Should I keep this appointment with strangers?* Ernst walked a few blocks before taking the U-Bahn home. He needed time to think.

I suspect Materne knew more about the deportations, far more than he was willing to tell my father. I imagine he had heard soldiers talk about Jews killed on trains by gas pumped through heating vents and mass executions in Polish villages. Materne probably knew the Nazis were fabricating lies about trains headed toward labor camps, lies to keep everyone ignorant of the truth.

Ernst made his way to the railway station to take the U-Bahn back home, to Kaiser Wilhelmstrasse, where he and his parents had lived for the past four years. Before that, they had rented an apartment on Linienstrasse 5, just a mile from Alexanderplatz, the commerce center of the city. They never wanted to move, but that decision was made by the government, not by them.

Among the many restrictions Hitler imposed after taking power, the "De-Judification of Living Space," allowed a landlord to evict a Jewish tenant for no reason. Once evicted, families were forced to find housing in "suitable neighborhoods."[6]

Ernst thought back to a day in 1939, shortly before they moved, when there was a bit of optimism, a brief moment when his family had shared excitement over the thought of leaving Germany. He and his parents had headed to the American consulate, his father carrying a large manila envelope. Wanting to make a good impression, his parents had dressed up for the occasion. Leopold wore a brown woolen suit with a crisp white shirt and a forest-green silk tie, and Betty had on her favorite dress, the navy blue one with white polka dots, along with a single-strand white pearl necklace.

Ernst and his parents stood on line at the American consulate, hoping their time had come to leave Germany. When Hitler was sworn in as chancellor, Berlin was home to 160,000 Jews. By 1939, emigration had brought Berlin's Jewish population down to 82,800.[7]

When the clerk called their names, the three walked up together and Leopold carefully spoke: "I've come here to request permission to immigrate. My son, my older son, Dr. Gerhard Joseph, lives in America, in Trenton, New Jersey. He is employed, and he has prepared an affidavit of support for me, my wife, and my son. Here, I have all the papers."

The foreign service officer opened the envelope, reviewed the documents, and after a few minutes that seemed to last forever, finally said, "Your son is willing to accept financial responsibility for all of you?"

Leopold nodded and quickly said, "Yes, that is correct."

"Well . . . the paperwork is in order."

There was a collective sigh of relief followed by Leopold's question, "Good, very good. So . . . when can we leave?"

"Not so fast, not so soon."

"But you just said the paperwork was OK."

"Herr Joseph," the gentleman at the desk explained, "there is a long list of people ahead of you. I can place you on the list, but your turn will not come soon. Go home. We'll let you know when it's your time."

Tragically, U.S. immigration policy limited the annual German quota at 27,000.[8] Antisemitism in the U.S., fear of immigrants taking away American jobs, and fear of German spies entering the country all contributed to the U.S. government's restricted immigration policy. With more than 200,000 people ahead of them, Leopold, Betty, and Ernst would have to wait many years before they could leave.

They walked out of the American consulate heartbroken and angry. When Gerhard left for America, the family hoped he would secure affidavits for them. And he did. But these documents were of no use. Why didn't President Franklin Roosevelt allow more Jews to enter? Why couldn't the American government raise the quota? Did Roosevelt not know of the situation facing Jews in Germany?

There was nothing more to do except wait for their number to be called. It never happened. In the summer of 1941, the American consulate closed down its office in Berlin, and by October, Hitler banned Jews from leaving. No hope of escape remained.

* * *

Ernst rode home on the U-Bahn and his mind drifted to Lilo, his girlfriend. He had met her two years ago at the theater, the Jewish theater. Ernst relaxed, knowing she was living with her former nanny, Klara and at least for now, she was safe. He thought about her wavy brown hair and her smile. Then he stopped himself. Not now, now he needed to concentrate on what to do.

Ernst thought about Materne's words: I found somebody who can help you and your parents. Ernst trusted Materne, never doubted his word, but what if Materne was being deceived? What if this stranger had fooled Materne?

Yet doing nothing meant deportation; the situation had become brutally clear. The Gestapo were coming into homes, and families were disappearing. Within weeks, if not days, their names would be on the list.

Ernst stepped off the train to walk the last few blocks home. He stopped to gaze at the stars, searching for familiar constellations. After a few minutes, his eyes found focus, and he smiled to see old friends. There was Polaris and, a bit in the distance, he spotted the twins, Gemini, with their two twinkling stars shining brightly in the night sky.

Betty was in the kitchen when Ernst entered the apartment. Usually, he walked in quietly, not wanting to answer his mother's unspoken questions. But tonight was different. Ernst came into the kitchen and said, "Finally, finally, I have good news."

Betty rushed to hug her son and listened as he said, "Now, we can pack our suitcase and stay together." Ernst looked down at his mother and forced himself to remove any lingering doubt.

3

EISENBAHNSTRASSE

"Herr Lippmann, Frau Lippmann, Ernst, come quickly, come quietly." Paul Pissarius spoke softly to the family he knew only by the name of Lippmann, not Joseph. He brought them into his three-and-a-half-room apartment on the ground floor on Eisenbahnstrasse 15. He opened a door to a small room, approximately 100 square feet, with a window facing out to the side courtyard.

Paul and Leni Pissarius lived in the Kreuzberg district of Berlin, a bit south of the city's center, a neighborhood of family owned and operated stores, modest apartments, commercial buildings, and factories. Their apartment building, an old, four-story structure, stood in a back courtyard, in the shadow of buildings directly facing the street.

Ernst viewed the room quickly. Pissarius had furnished it for them with beds and a small table. He looked at each of them and said, "The window must always remain covered, but light will still come through the curtain. It will be OK. Not so many people come by here."

The remote location of the building reassured Ernst, and that far outweighed the discomfort of the cramped space. He breathed deeply, relieved to have trusted Materne and to be in a safe place where no one could find them.

Pissarius added, "The bathroom is outside the apartment, down the hall. No one else lives on the ground floor, so the bathroom is only for us."

Ernst glanced over at his mother, afraid she would complain about sharing a bathroom. She could be a bit particular and fussy, but not now. He studied his parents as they silently looked at the room. It was small, but at least they could be together.

When Ernst and his parents took shelter on January 31, 1943, they entered the world of living underground. Living underground, sometimes called living illegal, meant not registering your name or address with the police; it meant hiding from the Gestapo. Officially, you ceased to exist.

The ration cards they had used were now useless. Pissarius provided food with his card and Leni's, and he relied on friends in the wholesale market who were willing to help.

Ernst knew that food would be a problem, but the urgent need for shelter eclipsed all other concerns. He had filled their suitcases with canned food and medicine for his father, but both would soon run out.

They passed the time listening to the sounds of footsteps in the courtyard, police sirens in the street, and aircraft flying overhead. Before going underground, Leopold had suffered heart problems and chest pains, and these symptoms continued intermittently. Hunger and fear were constant companions.

A few weeks after Ernst and his parents took shelter, Pissarius casually remarked, "So . . . we didn't throw you out after three days."

Ernst looked at him with a puzzled expression.

"Ah, I was sure Materne never told you."

Ernst still had no idea what Pissarius was saying.

"Ernst, when Materne first came to me looking for a hiding place, he said it would be for a very short time, just for three days. Of course, I never believed this crazy story of 'just for three days.' But you know Materne, he's a talker and will say anything. He needed to get you out of Kaiser Wilhelmstrasse. The police had your address. Materne knew, everyone knew, that a knock on your door would be coming soon. So, he made up a story of nonsense, pretending you would stay only a short time. Anyway, I first had to discuss with Leni."

Ernst sat stunned, taking in this new information. He had no idea that Materne had brought them here under the illusion of a brief stay. His mind started racing. *Is he telling me we have to leave? Where could we possibly go?*

Pissarius interrupted Ernst's worries, bringing him back to his conversation with Leni.

"So, I came home and told Leni what Materne said. She looked at me and laughed. 'Then what? What happens after three days? If we say yes to Materne, we do it right.'"

Pissarius paced around the room a few times and thought about his neighbors blindly following the Nazi doctrine. Then he stopped, looked at Leni, and said, "OK . . . we should do this."

Paul Pissarius, the youngest of eight children, five boys and three girls, grew up in a family of tradesmen. His father worked as a builder, and his brothers followed their father's lead by becoming skilled carpenters, locksmiths, and masons. The family home was near Eberswalde, 37 miles northeast of Berlin, a town with parks, lakes, and canals, a far cry from the crowds and culture of Berlin. Pissarius followed the family tradition and apprenticed as a carpenter. Later he worked as a salesman in Berlin, driving a horse and wagon to pick up merchandise in the Central Market Hall and peddling groceries to small businesses throughout the city.[1] He proudly served his country in the Great War, but now at age 48, his military days were over.

One day in mid-February, Betty woke up in the early morning hours, a bit groggy from a restless sleep. Not seeing her son, she shook her husband. "Leopold, wake up, wake up. Where is Ernst?" Leopold squinted in the dim light, looked around the tiny room with an expression that changed from confusion to fear. Betty put on her dress, stockings, shoes, and sweater, sat on the chair by the bed, and waited. Time seemed to pass so slowly; checking her watch frequently just made her worry more. She started to walk toward the window, wanting to peek outside, but held herself back and returned to the chair.

Hours later, Ernst returned. With relief Betty said, "Thank God you're back. Ernst, I was so worried." Then immediately added, "What happened? Why were you gone?"

Ernst took off his backpack, removed his scarf and overcoat, and said, "I'm sorry. I knew you would be worried. It's impossible for Pissarius to provide enough food for the five of us. His ration cards are not enough." He opened his backpack and took out a loaf of bread, a small container of margarine, and a few cans of fish. "I went to the market, to people we knew, people we trusted."

After that first time, Ernst began going out once a week, for coal to heat the apartment or for food or to see Lilo. That part of his life he kept private. He wondered if his mother guessed, but he never asked. Police were constantly patrolling the streets, subways, and railroad stations, demanding to see identification cards. Ernst timed his excursions for the early morning hours, before too many officers were on duty. Yet sometimes a confrontation was unavoidable.

My father died in 1972, on a cold, snowy day in February, and most of his days in hiding remain a mystery to me. He wrote down some of his recollections in longhand, in pencil, on the backs of other correspondence. He transferred the notes to sheets of typewritten words, and those sheets, now dogeared by time and my reading and rereading, have formed the background of this book. I believe my father thought about submitting his writing to a newspaper or magazine for publication. That never happened.

One of the events in his narrative revealed the risk of being on the street:

To avoid situations of danger, I walked through the streets of Berlin and tried to stay away from public transportation. But sometimes I had to use a streetcar or subway. I did the utmost to watch for any danger signs. On streetcars, I always placed myself near an entrance in order to leave the streetcar immediately, even if in motion, should it be necessary.

One day, I entered a newer streetcar with two compartments connected by a small middle piece. I placed myself next to the driver with the thought of getting out at the next stop. I never sat down. I was always standing, watching the people inside the car or entering. Shortly after I entered, we had to cross the Halensee Bridge. Standing next to the driver and looking out, I saw what I thought would be the end of me. Three policemen were standing in the middle of the bridge. One raised his arm, ordering all streetcars to stop. There was almost no other traffic on the bridge and not many people on the sidewalks. Two policemen remained outside when the streetcar stopped. One entered the car by the middle entrance. I did not turn around when I heard the policemen say: "All men, your identification cards, please."

I opened the door next to me, stepped off the streetcar and walked slowly to the sidewalk, expecting to be called back every second by the policemen standing on the bridge next to the street car. But nobody called me back. Did they not see me? No other person besides me was on the bridge. And they did not see me? I tried to walk normally, so as not to be noticed. Nothing happened. Silence.[2]

Deeply shaken by this close encounter, Ernst calmed his nerves and walked home. Luck protected him that day, and on the many other days he walked through the streets of Berlin. It was truly a game of chance.

* * *

When the war began, Allied pilots directed their bombs at military targets, but as the fighting continued, pilots took aim at factories throughout the city. Their intent was to reduce industrial production and, probably equally important, to

29

destroy enemy morale. The lives lost and homes reduced to rubble were not collateral damage; they were part of the military objective.

The apartment on Eisenbahnstrasse was a block away from DeTeWe, Deutsche Telephonwerke, a manufacturer of telephone and cable equipment, a factory targeted by the Allies. Each time the alarm sounded, Leni and Paul, along with their neighbors, ran into the *Luftschutzkeller*, the air raid shelter. But not those in hiding. Ernst and his parents stayed in the room, listened as planes flew overhead, and anxiously waited and prayed for the bombing to end. Their never-ending fear of being discovered was amplified with the sound of the siren.

One time the Allied bombs came extremely close. Betty sat stiffly in her chair by the wall, looked at her son, and said, "Ernst, listen, listen . . . something is wrong. The noise is getting louder and louder, never before was it so bad." Betty clasped her hands, squeezed her fingers, and rubbed her palms back and forth. "The planes are coming in, they're coming in closer."

Ernst stood still, wanting to hear the gradual abatement of the noise, but instead the sound steadily increased. "We stay close together, just like always, and we get through. Soon, soon, the planes will be gone." Ernst knew exactly what his mother was saying, but he wanted to ease her fear. He heard the searing sounds of approaching bombers as they flew directly overhead.

Ernst, Leopold, and Betty held on to each other, braced themselves against the wall as they felt the ground shaking. Moments later, the room was covered with debris and white dust from fallen plaster. The force of the explosion shattered the glass window and turned over the mattresses and chairs. Ernst looked at his parents, who were terrified and afraid to move but not injured. His relief at their narrow escape dissipated when he realized that the exterior wall, the one facing the courtyard, was badly damaged. The large ragged holes in the outside wall left them exposed.

In the nearby shelter, Paul sat next to Leni and heard the sounds of the planes intensify as they came in closer. Silently to himself, Paul repeated, *Our house won't be bombed. Our house won't be bombed.* Those were Leni's words, the words she had said when they first decided to shelter the Lippmann family. So far her words had held true.

As soon as the all clear siren rang, Leni and Paul rushed out to find their neighborhood reduced to rubble. Fire engines with sirens screaming found their way through streets covered in broken bricks and fallen tree limbs. Leni and Paul raced back home to find an exploded bomb lying in the courtyard. Their building had escaped a direct hit, but the outside wall was torn apart.

Seeing Ernst and his parents were unharmed, Leni kept her voice low. "Quickly, come with me," she said. "You can't stay there." Leni brought them into the parlor, away from neighbors with curious eyes and probing questions. The immediate need was privacy. Paul's early training as a carpenter now proved invaluable. He bartered his food coupons for wooden planks in the black market and restored the wall.

It was a miracle that all five escaped injury, the apartment building was still standing, and their secret remained intact. In this time when God seemed to be absent, when prayers went unheard and unanswered, there were a few moments when God appeared.

I have but one picture of Paul and Leni, one image to hold on to. It is dated 1946, after the war. They are standing outside, perhaps in a park, surrounded by trees and shrubbery. Paul, slender with thinning hair, stares directly into the camera, his arm around Leni's shoulder in a protective way. Leni, a pretty woman with soft waves framing her face, wears a flowered long-sleeve dress and smiles proudly as she stands next to her husband. These two people, who look rather ordinary, were true heroes.

Paul and Leni Pissarius, 1946, Berlin

4

THE JACOBY FAMILY

In 1932, Lilo Jacoby, a girl of nine, sat on the sofa in the living room on Hektorstrasse 19 in Berlin and traced the ragged edges of the hole in a silver cigarette case with her fingertips. Lilo, a petite child with brunette curls, sat very still and turned the silver case round and round and tried to imagine the past. She handed it back to her father, Bruno Jacoby, and with a gentle nod, he tucked the tarnished and dented case, his lucky charm, inside the breast pocket of his jacket. Bruno had served with distinction during the Great War and earned the Iron Cross, First Class, but he spoke little about his wartime experiences. All Lilo knew was that this case had caught a bullet and saved her father's life.

Lilo pulled down a framed photo from the bookshelf, a photograph of her father wearing a jacket, vest, and striped tie. He looked serious, not at all the way she thought of him. In the photo, Lilo could see the ribbons of the Iron Cross on his jacket lapel. She knew how proud her father was of the medal. It was a sign of loyalty and patriotism. He considered himself as German as any of his neighbors, and he believed they regarded him the same way.

Bruno Jacoby

Lilo often heard her father talk about politics, how glad he was that Paul von Hindenburg was re-elected president in the 1932 election rather than that miserable Adolf Hitler. "See Lilo," he said, "the German people are smart. They don't want Hitler."

And while Hitler was never elected, Hindenburg did appoint him chancellor on January 30, 1933. At that time, communists were gaining more control in parliament, and many Germans looked to the Nazi party to hold back communism. Subsequent events, including the Reichstag fire and the passage of Enabling laws, allowed Hitler to issue laws without parliament's approval, transforming Germany from a democracy to a dictatorship. The final step came in August 1934 when Hindenburg died, and Hitler declared himself the absolute leader, the Führer.

Bruno always regarded Hitler as a crazy man with outlandish ideas, a man who would soon be thrown out of office. He trusted his wartime service to protect his family. For a while, it did.

* * *

Bruno Jacoby loved the theater and, as a young man, performed in Shakespeare's *King Lear*. He often quoted passages from Friedrich Schiller's play *Wilhelm Tell*, and he passed his love for theater to his daughter Lilo. Bruno had another daughter, an older child, Anna Marie, from his first marriage before the war. Lilo knew that her father's first wife was an actress and that she was not Jewish, but not why the marriage failed. Anna Marie was raised as a Christian in her mother's home in Munich, and she also knew her father was Jewish.

When Bruno came home after the war, he transitioned from an actor to a journalist and wrote theater reviews for a major German newspaper, the *Berliner Tageblatt*. In 1921, Bruno married Ella Davidsohn, a young woman from Cammin, in the district of Stettin, a small town in northern Germany near the Baltic Sea. The population of Cammin was predominantly Protestant, with a Jewish minority of less than one percent.[1] Ella's father was a cantor, and she had grown up celebrating Jewish holidays and traditions. Ella had just one sibling, a brother, Martin, whom she adored. Martin intended to enter the university and prepare for a career in law, but those plans were put on hold with the outbreak of the Great War. Ella spoke with deep sorrow about the last time she had seen her brother. In the autumn of 1918, he had come home for a brief visit, proudly dressed in his soldier's uniform. The war was going badly for Germany, and everyone believed the end was near. Ella's mother begged Martin to stay home, but how could a young man of courage and honor listen to such a request? Martin returned to the battlefield and was killed a few weeks before Germany surrendered on November 11, 1918.

* * *

My mother has told me this story so often, and to me, his death echoes the narrative of *All Quiet on the Western Front* by Erich Maria Remarque. In the novel, Remarque describes the mental and physical challenge of young men facing combat, their transition from boys filled with patriotic optimism to weary soldiers. I recognized Martin in Remarque's poignant description of a soldier home on leave and his vulnerability on return to battle.

* * *

Bruno and Ella lived in an apartment on Hektorstrasse 19 in the Charlottenburg-Wilmersdorf district, the western section of Berlin. The apartment was on the top floor of a four-story building, a block from Kurfürstendamm.

Bruno was a sociable man who enjoyed going out with his wife to the theater and having friends at the house for a game of cards. Bruno and Ella celebrated "German holidays" with Christmas trees and Easter baskets, and somehow Ella forgot about Hanukkah menorahs and seder plates.

It was 1921, when Ella was 33, rather late for a first-time mother, that she gave birth to a son, Hans Martin Herman, named in memory of her beloved brother. Two years later, on July 21,1923, Ella had her second child, Elisabeth Charlotte Lina. Three first names were quite fashionable at the time, but soon the name shortened to Lilo.

Lilo's closest ally, her best friend and buddy, was her brother. Hans Martin was an outgoing young boy who spoke to everyone and turned strangers into friends. For Hans, riding a bike was part of daily life, even if it meant a couple of spills, a few bruised knees, and many torn trousers.

One morning Lilo looked out the front window and called out, "Vati, come quick. See that garbage truck? Who is that riding on the side, waving his hand?"

Bruno laughed and said, "Lilo, you know who that is. Wave back. Hans is having a grand time."

Lilo waved and sighed, a bit jealous of her brother's grand adventure. As the garbage truck passed by, blasting its horn, Lilo nodded her head and smiled.

Hans Martin included Lilo in sports and games, sometimes forgetting that she was a bit younger and smaller than him. One day at Wellenbad, the popular wave pool in Berlin, he challenged his sister, saying, "Lilo, come and jump off the high dive with me."

"No, Hans," Lilo answered. "It's way too high. Go yourself."

Hans persisted. "Lilo, what if we go together? We climb up, I hold your hand, and then we both jump?"

Still not too sure about this idea, but not wanting to be teased as a coward, Lilo agreed.

They walked to the edge of the board, and Hans said, "Lilo, listen, I'll count 'one, two, three,' and then we jump. Don't let go of my hand."

Hans, larger and heavier, fell straight down. Lilo, who never let go, rotated to a horizontal position and hit the water hard, with a loud smack. A crowd of onlookers came rushing over and watched Lilo slowly climb out with a bright pink belly and a stinging pain she would long remember.

There was one activity that Lilo did without Hans: ballet. Twice a week Lilo stood straight and tall by the barre, stretched out her fingers until her muscles twitched, and held the position longer than any of the other girls. She loved the graceful moves of the ballerina and dreamed of performing on stage. Lilo had a natural grace, and her teachers encouraged her, even suggesting she enroll in a special school for dance. Bruno would hear none of this. Lilo's education would follow the same path as Hans's did, at the primary school, the *Grundschule*.

Lilo dancing, age 10

Lilo started school at age six, the way it began for all German children. Each morning, Lilo and Hans Martin walked together a few blocks to the neighborhood school, and then entered separate classrooms for boys and girls. In the early school years, the pre-Hitler days, Lilo never felt antisemitism, never heard antisemitic slurs or experienced hostile behavior from classmates or neighbors.

There is a photo of Hans Martin on his first day of school. He is properly dressed in short pants, with a double-breasted overcoat, high socks, laced shoes, a bag over his left shoulder, and another one on his back. In his right hand, he holds on tightly to a pair of gloves. His left arm rests on a large cone. This cone, a *Schultüte*, is filled with sweets, typically given on the first day of school. His cap is a bit large and partially hides his face, which shows a trace of uncertainty.

Perhaps he's thinking about who his teachers will be or perhaps about eating some of the chocolates.

Hans Martin Jacoby, 1928

At the age of ten, after primary school was completed, the German education system divided children into two tracks: a vocational path and an academic path. The academic path brought boys to a gymnasium and girls to a lyceum. At the start of 1933, Hans Martin was a student at the Grunewald Gymnasium and Lilo was at the *Grundschule*. Lilo expected to enter the Bismarck Lyceum in the fall.

That spring, a group of girls huddled together in the elementary school courtyard. They had been buddies since age six, the year they entered school. Lilo was friends with all the girls. They liked her. She was good at sports, loved to dance, and had a good-looking older brother. She heard them talking about the upcoming summer vacation and then starting school together at the Bismarck Lyceum.

As Lilo approached, the group became quiet. After a few minutes, one of the girls said, "They might not let you in."

"What are you talking about? I passed the entrance exam, just like you."

No one answered. No one looked at her. Lilo walked away, confused by the strange interaction. She ran home, up the stairs to the apartment on the top floor, and called out for her mother.

Ella hugged her daughter, held her hands, and tried to explain. "Lilo, you and Hans can stay in school, but so much is changing. Many Jewish children will not be going back."

A law had passed in April against overcrowding in schools. "Overcrowding" was a misleading term. There was no concern over the number of students per classroom, only the number of Jewish students. At the time the law was passed, Hitler had been chancellor for just three months, and many Germans had not embraced the antisemitic Nazi doctrine. To show respect to Jewish soldiers, and to honor their service, children whose fathers had fought in the Great War were allowed to remain in school.[2]

However, that year, in which Hitler came to power, marked the beginning of persecution against Jews that would lead to atrocities no one could have imagined. It was the year Bruno was forced out of his job writing theater reviews. He continued earning a living as a traveling salesman, selling advertisement space for the paper.

Lilo sat still for a long time, frightened and confused by all the new rules. Her father wasn't worried, yet Lilo could sense her mother was. But then again, she was always worried about something.

In the fall, Lilo entered the Bismarck Lyceum along with her grammar school friends. She loved learning French, and much preferred its melodious tones over German. Lilo imagined future romances and practiced saying, "*Je t'aime,*" clearly more elegant than "*Ich liebe dich.*"

Each morning while waiting in the courtyard for the school doors to open, Lilo carefully scanned the approaching cars. She watched the large black Mercedes sedan slowly approach the front door. A chauffeur opened the back door and out stepped Eva Cassirer, a petite girl with straight blond hair, cut just below her chin. She wore elegant clothes and shoes and carried a monogramed leather school bag. Lilo was fascinated by Eva, but Eva, three years older and part of a different social circle, was only an acquaintance.

I had the opportunity to see the Bismarck Lyceum in May 1995. It was my initial trip to Germany, and Mom's first return to a country filled with painful memories. We were there in the early afternoon, but the students had already gone home, and the courtyard was quiet. I asked Mom what she remembered.

"We used to march in a big circle, round and round," Mom replied, looking up at the building and the heavy wooden entrance doors.

"Was that like recess or Phys Ed?"

"No, there weren't any games, like you had in school. We just marched around. We were outside to get fresh air. That's all."

"And what about your classroom? How was it inside?" I asked, hoping to get more information.

"It was strict. We had to sit with our hands folded on the table, and we would stand when a teacher entered the room."

The school, now named the Sophie-Charlotte Oberschule, is a secondary school for girls and boys. While the outside looks the same as when Mom was a student, the website describes a modern school with the expected curriculum in science, math, German, and English, plus required courses in ethics and clubs focused on refugee assistance and climate protection. The painful past of Nazi Germany is not forgotten, as reflected in the school's guiding principle:

Know what happened before us
Understand what is happening today,
Gain orientation for the future.
Learn for a life
of freedom and tolerance
on the foundation of human rights.

* * *

As a young girl, Lilo felt safe and protected at school and home, but this wall of security was paper-thin. Not only were there anti-Jewish laws, but Joseph Goebbels, the master of propaganda, used newspapers, radio, and speeches to reinforce the image of a Jew as the enemy. Propaganda was a powerful tool to win support from the German public and create an atmosphere tolerant of violence against Jews.

Most dramatic were the Nuremberg rallies, gigantic events orchestrated to stir up patriotic fervor and strike fear among those on the outside: Gypsies, communists, and especially Jews. Hundreds of thousands of party members, along with the Hitler

Youth, came to Nuremberg, listened to speeches, and marched through the streets carrying Nazi flags and banners as crowds cheered in support of a strong German military power.

Three new laws were announced at the 1935 rally. The first proclaimed the swastika flag as the flag of Germany. The second denied Jews their citizenship and their right to vote. The third prohibited marriage between Germans and Jews.

To implement these laws, the Nazis defined a Jew as a person with three or more Jewish grandparents. This simple definition was based on ancestry, on birth or baptismal records of grandparents. To deal with the thousands of Germans who had one or two Jewish grandparents, the term *Mischling*, half-breed, was adopted. A person with two Jewish grandparents was labeled a half Jew, or Mischling first degree; a person with one Jewish grandparent was labeled a quarter Jew, or Mischling second degree.[3]

These laws had a direct impact on Anna Marie, Bruno's oldest child. After his divorce, Bruno continued seeing Anna Marie, who spent time in Berlin with him every summer. Lilo's relationship with Anna Marie, ten years her senior, was cordial, never close. When Anna Marie was in her early twenties, she fell in love with a Nazi officer. Even though Anna Marie was raised by a Christian mother, the Nuremberg Laws labeled her a Mischling first degree and unfit to marry a Nazi officer. When her marriage application was denied, Anna Marie wrote angry letters to her father, blaming him for her unhappiness. Lilo watched her father read Anna Marie's bitter words and, with deep sadness in his eyes, carefully fold the papers and set them aside.

* * *

Who is a Jew? This question stayed in my mother's mind long after the war ended. She would frequently ask me, "Is a Jew defined by race or religion?" This is a terribly difficult question, one that scholars have written volumes on and extensively debated. While I never knew how to answer, I wasn't troubled by the question the way Mom was. Growing up in New Jersey in the 1950s, I experienced a world that allowed for ambiguity and conversation. How we lived and what we believed were as important as who our grandparents were. But in Germany, the question, "Who is a Jew?" was asked often and with serious consequences.

When I was in elementary school, I asked to wear a necklace with a Star of David. We lived in Hamilton Township, an area outside of Trenton, with lots of Italian families. Many kids wore gold crosses, but Mom wouldn't let me wear the Jewish star. The message was clear: don't advertise that you're Jewish.

In 1935, it no longer mattered that Bruno Jacoby had served with distinction in the Great War. When the doors to the Bismarck Lyceum and the Grunewald Gymnasium closed to her children, Ella searched for an alternative. She had a cousin, Dr. Bernard Zucker, a teacher at the Lessler Schule, a private Jewish school for girls. With this family connection, the school accepted Lilo at reduced tuition, an important consideration at the time. But Ella could not find a place for her son.

It was Hans Martin himself who found a solution, a temporary one. With characteristic optimism, he came home and announced he had found work at Café Dobrin on Kurfürstendamm. The café, owned by a Jewish couple, was a popular place to linger and chat with friends over a cup of hot coffee. Hans Martin assured his mother that soon, very soon, he would return to school.

That fall, twelve-year-old Lilo walked through the entrance door of Lessler Schule and came face to face with a portrait of a man with a long, curly, dark beard, bushy eyebrows, deep-set brown eyes, and a penetrating stare. Lilo had no idea who he was. In every classroom the teachers spoke of the man in the portrait, Theodor Herzl, and his Zionist message. Many of her classmates knew about him and spoke eagerly of their families' plans to immigrate to Palestine. Quietly Lilo thought, *Palestine? It's a desert. My father would never go there.* He wants to stay in Germany, nowhere else.

Theodor Herzl, an Austrian Jewish journalist, grew up believing antisemitism could be erased through assimilation. His views completely changed after he covered the trial of Alfred Dreyfus, a Jewish French artillery officer, falsely accused and wrongly imprisoned for treason, passing military secrets to Germany. At the trial, Herzl heard crowds in the street calling, "Death to the traitor! Death to the Jews." Witnessing their collective anger against all Jews, Herzl abandoned his position on assimilation and became a fierce supporter of Zionism, urging Jews to immigrate to Palestine with the goal of creating a Jewish state.

After the trial, new evidence emerged linking a different French officer to the crime. Most probably this information would never have received recognition were it not for the French novelist Émile Zola, who wrote a passionate letter, *J'accuse!*, that appeared on the front page of a Parisian newspaper. Zola accused the French government and army of obstruction of justice, religious prejudice, and using the press to wrongfully convict Dreyfus. *J'accuse!* became a rallying call in defense of Dreyfus. A year later, Dreyfus was pardoned and set free.

The Lessler Schule gave Lilo an education in Zionism and Judaism, but the heart of her identity as a Jew came elsewhere. Her personal connection to God and Judaism came from Joachim Prinz, a young, handsome, energetic, and charismatic rabbi in Berlin.

Rabbi Prinz delivered sermons at Friedenstempel, a synagogue just a block away from Lilo's house on Hektorstrasse. Even before Hitler came to power, Prinz spoke out against National Socialism and warned of its impending danger. His sermons blended political events with traditional Jewish teaching and a strong Zionist message. Rabbi Prinz instilled an intense Jewish pride in his congregation, even if he disregarded a few rules, such as driving on Shabbat. Prinz recognized how assimilated his cosmopolitan Berlin congregants were, how strongly they identified as German patriots, and how they discounted the depth of antisemitism in Germany. He delivered strong warnings of the imminent danger of Hitler and urged his congregation not to dismiss Hitler's evil message.

Bruno and Ella had been *Drei-Tage-Juden*, three-day-Jews, who attended services only on the two days of Rosh Hashanah and Yom Kippur. But whenever Rabbi Prinz spoke, they always stood in line along with hundreds of others, waiting for the doors to open.

Lilo, Hans Martin, and many other teenagers spent Shabbat afternoons at the rabbi's home. Rabbi Prinz ate lunch and played ball with them in the afternoon, something no other rabbi did. Praying and studying Torah were traditionally part of Shabbat; playing ball was not. Orthodox rabbis criticized Rabbi

Prinz. The kids loved him. Prinz taught them Jewish history, prayers, and songs, and gave them a community of warmth. Together, they sang "Hine Ma Tov":

> *Hine ma tov u'ma-nayim*
> *Shevet ach-im gam ya-chad*
> How good and pleasant it is
> For brothers and sisters to sit together.

During that time, Lilo learned to read Hebrew, to chant the prayers for Shabbat, and to sing Hatikva. Through the influence of Rabbi Prinz, Hans urged his father to celebrate only Hanukkah and give up Christmas. Bruno listened. Santa Claus stopped coming to the house, and a Christmas tree no longer stood in the parlor.

Yet Hans could not convince his father to consider leaving Germany. Bruno was then a man in his late fifties. He had earned a living through writing, through the German language, and he worried he would not have the skills to find employment elsewhere. Bruno still believed this terrible time would pass, and he could not bring himself to uproot his family and begin all over.

With his outspoken words against Hitler, Rabbi Prinz attracted the attention of the Gestapo. They monitored his speeches and writing and frequently brought him in for interrogation. Fearing possible arrest, Rabbi Prinz, along with his wife and children, packed up their suitcases and immigrated to America in 1937. Lilo was crushed by his departure and a bit surprised that Rabbi Prinz had chosen America over Palestine. Other rabbis came to Friedenstempel, but for Lilo, no one replaced the energy, the spirit and the charisma of Rabbi Prinz.

* * *

I never meet this rabbi my mother adored, but I know he created a powerful second chapter in his life as a civil rights and religious leader. My friend Sally Steinberg-Brent was a member of Rabbi Prinz's congregation at Temple B'nai Abraham in Newark, New Jersey. A few years ago, I walked into Sally's home in Princeton and noticed a framed photo of Rabbi Prinz and Dr. Martin Luther King Jr. hanging above the grand piano. Sally explained that Rabbi Prinz had been her teacher in Hebrew high school, and she spoke with a tone of admiration that echoed my mother's voice.

"Rabbi Prinz introduced me to Dr. King, and I got his autograph," Sally proudly said and then pointed out the program card with King's signature. "He came to the synagogue as a guest speaker. It was in the early 1960s."

"Did Rabbi Prinz speak with a German accent?" I asked.

"No, not at all. He had more of a British accent."

"Oh, that's surprising." I thought of how Mom had never lost her accent, which was quite obvious to everyone except me. I could hear her accent in telephone messages, but face to face, I never heard it.

I asked Sally what she remembered about Rabbi Prinz.

"His dedication to social justice. You know, he spoke at the March on Washington in 1963 with Dr. King."

"I remember seeing photos of Rabbi Prinz at the march, but I don't remember what he said."

"Nobody does," Sally replied.

"What do you mean?" I asked. "Why not?"

"It was a great speech, but immediately afterwards, Dr. King stood up and delivered an even greater speech."

I found Rabbi Prinz's speech on YouTube and listened as he spoke of his experience in Nazi Germany and urged the crowd to speak up in the face of prejudice. "Bigotry and hatred are not the most urgent problems. The most shameful and the most tragic problem is silence."[4] When Rabbi Prinz finished speaking, Dr. King stood up and, in a booming voice that reached thousands of people gathered at the civil rights rally, delivered his iconic "I Have a Dream" speech.

When Rabbi Prinz retired in 1977, Mom was living in Ewing Township. I never realized that Rabbi Prinz was in Newark, just sixty miles away. Mom and I could have taken a car ride, driven up the New Jersey Turnpike and walked into Temple B'nai Abraham. Not that difficult, but it never happened.

In 1937, there were many changes for Lilo. She was fourteen and no longer at the Lessler Schule. She had found a job as a photographer's assistant at the Atelier von Santho. The studio was in the same building as Café Dobrin, where Hans Martin worked, a nice coincidence. Her job was to set up the lights as Santho directed. He photographed models in elegant designer outfits, and his photos appeared in the high-fashion magazines of the time, *Die Dame* and *Der Silberspiegel*. Santho was a man who loved fashion and slept with many of the models, a secret Lilo never shared at home.

Her next job was at a marzipan factory. While the surroundings were not glamorous, the paycheck was important to the family.

Lilo continued to live the life of a teenage girl, meeting friends for ice cream at Olivaer Platz, talking about hairstyles and clothes, and daydreaming about Hans Peter Messerschmidt. He was her brother's friend, but lately he had started paying attention to her. He was rather tall, so Lilo always insisted that he walk in the street next to her, while she walked on the curb to gain a few inches. Hans Peter was outgoing and funny, and Lilo enjoyed his attention.

The world outside was changing rapidly and the depth of antisemitism in Germany became clear on November 9, 1938.

My mom often spoke to me about that night, about seeing her synagogue in flames. In November 1988, on the fiftieth anniversary of Kristallnacht, Mom shared those memories at my synagogue, The Jewish Center in Princeton. A packed congregation sat silent, listening to this short lady who stood on a step stool to reach the podium tell her story:

I was only fifteen years old at that time, but it is still so clear in my mind, as if it happened yesterday. I woke up in the middle of the night from the noise of broken glass, shouts, and screams. I climbed out of my bed, went to the window, and saw how the Nazis smashed all the windows in Jewish shops, homes, and buildings.

Our house was not too far from our synagogue, called Friedenstempel, which means House of Peace. I saw through my window a ball of fire coming out of the synagogue. Oh my God! They destroyed everything, burned the Torah scrolls, arks, curtains, prayer books. Everything went to flames. But that was not all.

I saw how people, young and old, were beaten with sticks and stones. I saw them lying in the street. I heard them scream.

Then my parents came to my room and told me that my brother Hans did not come home that night. He was seventeen years old and full of life. We were all afraid he might be killed.[5]

Hans had gone out that evening with friends. When he saw the flames from the synagogue, he realized it was too dangerous to be out on the street. He spent the night in an empty building and safely returned home the next morning.

* * *

There was one argument between her parents that Lilo always remembered. Most of the time, Ella went along with Bruno, except over one issue.

Ella desperately wanted the children to be on the Kindertransport, a program set up by the British government to bring Jewish children, ages one to seventeen, to Great Britain. The program, started immediately after Kristallnacht, brought children, unaccompanied by their parents, to foster homes, hostels, and farms. The first transport left Berlin with two hundred children in December 1938.

Ella pleaded with her husband to let the children go, but Bruno wouldn't hear of it. "We stay together, nothing will happen to us." This argument continued for days. Ella knew her husband would never leave Germany, but here was an opportunity to save the children, yet he still would not agree.

The anti-Jewish laws continued, and in April 1939, when the "De-Judification of Living Space" came into effect, the Jacoby family was forced out of their home on Hektorstrasse. They moved to a smaller apartment, in a "Jewish house" on Potsdamer Strasse 198, owned by a family friend, Herr Bruno Warschauer, an elderly gentleman who used a wheelchair. The new apartment was in a commercial area of the city, on a busy street where residential and office buildings stood next to one another. It was not as nice as Hektorstrasse.

On September 1, 1939, Germany marched across the border into Poland, and two days later, France and Great Britain declared war on Germany. World War II began with the swift and devastating invasion into Poland. The Luftwaffe, the German air force, attacked roads and railroads, with massive bombings on Warsaw, killing tens of thousands of civilians. In mid-September, Germany's ally, the Soviet Union, invaded eastern Poland, and by month's end, Poland was defeated.

As the Wehrmacht advanced through Europe, the Nazi government ordered Jews to work *Zwangsarbeit*, forced labor, to support military operations. In mid-June 1940, Lilo began working at Siemens Charlottenburg Ufer, the factory by the Spree River. "I would sit on a small chair and put little wires, red and green ones, into holes," she told me many years later. "And there was an iron, you know, to heat up the wires. I had to do it quickly, before more wires came."

Hitler had now been in power for more than seven years, and he had succeeded in creating a Nazi regime that degraded Jews in speeches and newspapers, banned Jewish students from schools, evicted Jews from their homes, and destroyed Jewish property. Despite all the layers of persecution, the Jews of Berlin found comfort and solace from one another and from the Jüdische Kulturbund, the Jewish cultural organization.

Hans Martin came often to the Kulturbund with his girlfriend, Susie, but when she couldn't make it, he brought Lilo along. Lilo, now seventeen, loved going to a concert or play. Along with listening to the music, she enjoyed dressing up, engaging in lighthearted conversations, flirting a bit, and forgetting about the outside world.

Though it sounds strange, the Kulturbund served the needs of both Jews and Nazis. The organization had been conceived from the vision of a few Jewish leaders, primarily Kurt Singer, the former opera director of the Berlin State Theater. When Nazi regulations forced all Jews in civil service jobs to retire, musicians and actors employed in state theaters found themselves unemployed.

Dr. Singer imagined a theater financed by the Jewish community, a place where Jewish performers could earn a living through their talent. To transform this idea into reality, he needed permission from Nazi officials. Dr. Singer, a veteran of the Great War and a man of considerable charm, charisma, and persuasion, submitted a plan to State Commissioner Hans Hinkel, an SS officer and head of the Prussian Theater Commission.

Hinkel recognized its benefit, not for the Jews but for the Nazis. Unemployed Jewish artists would receive a paycheck from other Jews and not be a burden to the state. And the theater would effectively segregate Jewish performers and keep them off the German stage.

In July 1933, the Nazi regime approved the creation of a Jewish theater. Attending a performance at the Kulturbund gave Jews an opportunity to laugh at the familiar lines in Shakespeare's *A Midsummer Night's Dream*, to listen to the spirited arias of

Mozart's *Marriage of Figaro* and the melancholy tones of Tchaikovsky's *Pathétique*, and to briefly enjoy a life that was rapidly changing. The Jüdische Kulturbund also gave the German government a vehicle of propaganda. It created a facade to the outside world that Jews in Germany were well treated.

The theater offered jobs to hundreds of unemployed Jews, including Bruno Jacoby, who sold theater tickets and wrote reviews. It allowed Bruno to remain connected to the world he loved.

My parents met at the Kulturbund in the winter of 1941. I know the story well. My dad loved classical music, and he came often to hear a live performance of a Bach sonata or a Schubert symphony. A pretty girl with shoulder-length wavy chestnut-brown hair and hazel eyes caught his attention. It took weeks before he approached her, as she was always talking and laughing with a young man. When he learned that the young man was her brother, Dad introduced himself and Mom replied, "I'm Elisabeth Charlotte Lena Jacoby, but that's way too many names for one person. Everyone calls me Lilo."

Their early dates were at the Tiergarten, a sprawling park in the heart of Berlin, with the iconic monument the Victory Column off in the distance. The linden trees were in blossom, with their pale yellow flowers tucked in between bright green leaves. There was a honey-and-lemon fragrance in the air. Ernst had fallen in love with Lilo, not just with her beauty but with her charm and optimism, and her power to chase away the darkness that permeated daily life.

But Lilo had reservations. There was a large age gap—she was seventeen and he was twenty-five—and for Lilo's tastes, Ernst was a bit too serious and old-fashioned. Yet, as Lilo rationalized, there weren't many other young men available. For the time, Ernst would do.

In the summer of 1941, before the deportations began, Ernst and Lilo, two different people, developed a relationship. When Ernst brought Lilo home to meet his parents, she found the apartment on Kaiser Wilhelmstrasse dark and gloomy and Herr Joseph rather cold. Everything was in sharp contrast to her family and, in Lilo's opinion, inferior. When Lilo introduced Ernst to her family, Hans was not impressed.

"Lilo, why are you going out with that old man? What do you see in him?" Hans asked his sister.

"Lilo, did you see his clothes? His shoes? He's even starting to lose his hair, like an old man."

Lilo's father and brother were critical of this new boyfriend. Not only were his clothes outdated, but more important, he lacked the social skills they valued. Ernst didn't drink or smoke, and he rarely smiled.

Despite their criticisms, Lilo continued to see him. During the long summer days, they rode the train to the outskirts of the city and spent weekend afternoons on a rowboat in the Havel River. There were picnic lunches and walks along the riverbanks, with the noise of Nazi stormtroopers far in the distance.

On September 11, 1941, the Gestapo closed down the Kulturbund, leaving those working there, including Bruno Jacoby, unemployed.

More surprising than its demise is that the Kulturbund lasted eight years. When it ended, the Nazis were well into carrying out plans for the annihilation of Jews in Europe. The German army had already invaded the Soviet Union, and special units,

Einsatzgruppen, had murdered Jews, gypsies, and communists in eastern Europe. There was no longer any need to pretend that Jews in Berlin were well treated.

Deportations from Berlin began in October 1941, with the first trains headed for the Lodz ghetto in Poland. Through the remaining months of the year, about ten thousand Jews were deported from Berlin to camps and ghettos in Lodz and Riga, Latvia.[6] Those remaining in Berlin did not know the fate of their relatives and friends. If they knew, some might have tried to resist; others might have attempted suicide.

The SS created the illusion that Jews were being brought to work camps. Bruno expected he and Ella would face physical labor, which would not be easy for a man of sixty-three and a woman of fifty-four. The best he could hope for was to remain strong until the war ended, until Hitler was defeated. He never imagined the truth.

Lilo and Hans Martin were at work that day in September 1942 when the Gestapo came to their house. Bruno and Ella were not as fortunate. The Gestapo walked in the same way they came to every other home. They knocked on the door. They entered with orders for Bruno and Ella to pack their suitcase and depart for resettlement in the east.

When Lilo and Hans Martin returned home, they found the front door sealed and a note posted ordering them to report to the deportation center on Grosse Hamburger Strasse. Lilo shut her eyes to stop the tears. She wiped her face and quietly repeated the words her parents said so often: "If they come for us, don't worry. We will be back. When this terrible time is over, we'll be together again."

Elisabeth and Hans Martin, about 1937

Hans Martin Jacoby, 1942

5

ALONE

Lilo and Hans broke the seal and entered the apartment. They crawled on the floor with the lights off, like robbers, intruders into their own home. They knew every inch so well, where the sofa stood, where the worn-out chair against the window sat and the turn in the hallway that led to the bedrooms. Lilo and Hans took some photos and a few pieces of jewelry. They could not stay long. The risk of being caught was too great.

They walked quickly to Klara Paschke's apartment on Knesebeckstrasse, more than a mile from Hektorstrasse. Klara had worked for the family for many years, but her employment ended when the children no longer needed a nanny, and the family could no longer afford a maid. Ella often invited Klara back to the house for coffee, and Klara doted on Lilo and Hans since she had no children of her own. Time and time again, she told them, "If something goes wrong, you come to me."

Klara understood when she saw Lilo and Hans Martin at the door and brought them in, saying, "I was afraid this was coming." She was a middle-aged German hausfrau, with her hair braided in a long single plait down her back. Klara's husband, a taxicab driver, accepted these two young adults in the house without question.

Twice, in the early morning hours when few people were walking the street, Lilo and Hans slipped back into their old apartment. They removed the police tape crisscrossed over the front door and entered silently, trying not to step on creaky floorboards. They took what could fit in their pockets, the gold ring with the oval amethyst stone, a coral necklace, and a silver soup spoon monogrammed with their mother's initials, E. D., Ella Davidsohn. After a few minutes, they carefully replaced the police tape and left. Hans returned by himself for a third time and found the door no longer sealed. He stopped, afraid to enter. Was this a trap? Would an alarm sound if he opened the door? Hans turned around, walked down the stairs, and never returned.

According to the notice that had been posted on the door when their parents were taken, Ella and Bruno Jacoby had been brought to the Jewish old-age home on Grosse Hamburger Strasse. The building had been transformed into a holding center. When enough people were assembled, they were loaded onto trains and taken away.

The last time Lilo and Hans entered the apartment, Lilo picked up an envelope off the floor, glanced at it, then tucked it away into her pocket. It was from Anna Marie, Bruno's daughter from his first marriage. Lilo waited to return to the safety of Klara's home before ripping it open. Tears welled up as she read the words. "Hans, come look at this."

"I don't want to see it," Hans replied. "Why should I read her words? Every letter she wrote was mean and spiteful."

"Hans, this letter is different, nothing like those other ones."

The previous letters were filled with angry words and bitterness towards their father. This was a note of apology. Anna Marie explained that her engagement to the Nazi officer was broken. She pleaded for forgiveness for the pain she had caused. Lilo cried reading words that would have comforted her father and eased his mind.

Hans read the note and angrily said, "This came too late. Now, she writes this?"

"Hans, do you think we can possibly get this letter to Vati?" Lilo asked.

Hans looked at his sister, knowing how dangerous that would be, yet also seeing her face streaked with tears.

"OK, we try."

They walked four miles to reach Grosse Hamburger Strasse and stood across the street from the assembly site where their parents were being held. Lilo held the letter tightly in her pocket. There were guards on patrol at the entrance, preventing anyone from leaving and questioning anyone approaching. Lilo and Hans stood in the shadows of the building and waited there quietly for a long time. They were nineteen and twenty-one years old, but they felt like children, lost and frightened. They wanted to reach out to their parents, touch their faces, hold their hands, and give them this note, but it was impossible. Yet how could they leave, how could they walk away? Finally, and for the last time, they caught a glimpse of their father and mother through a window in the old-age home. Lilo wrapped her fingers around the letter deep in her pocket, locked arms with her brother, and as they walked away, she cried softly and repeated, "They will be back, when this terrible war is over, they will be back."

My mother has told me this story so often. That moment is deeply etched in her mind, frozen in time and layered with pain. It leaves me unable to do anything to comfort her but simply listen. I can't take away the pain. All I can do is write words to preserve the past and remember my grandparents, whom I never met.

* * *

The first train from the Jewish old-age home left Grosse Hamburger Strasse in June 1942 with forty-six residents plus four from the medical staff. Three of the passengers were over eighty-five years old; the oldest was a ninety-five-year-old woman.[1] It is heartbreaking to picture these elderly, frail people walking onto the train, obeying the Nazi orders.

After the initial deportation, three more transports followed in rapid succession. A total of 187 residents, including fifteen people over the age of eighty-five, were taken. When Bruno and Ella were deported on September 5, 1942, they left a site where people were sleeping on the floor or on bags filled with straw, a site with dreadful sanitary conditions. They walked onto a train that took them to an unspeakable end.

There are very few firsthand accounts of life inside the assembly site, but in a collection of writings about the conditions of concentration camps, there is a letter written by Mathilde Bing, a forty-four-year-old woman, that conveys the despair of being detained at Grosse Hamburger Strasse:

My dear friend, this might be the last letter. There are constant rumors that we will be moved tomorrow. Then it might start any day. [. . .] I try to think from just one hour to the next. You have to close yourself off entirely. Otherwise the terrible misery about us will make one utterly sick. The day before yesterday a man died of TB in the next room. [. . .] Yesterday, a man committed suicide. [. . .] I do not want to give up hope until the end, but my mind knows precisely that this is the end.[2]

Soon after Bruno and Ella were deported, a postcard came to Klara's home. It was a handwritten note from Bruno, telling the children they were on a train, going east, but where he did not know. Bruno ended the short note saying not to worry. The card was postmarked Theresienstadt. One card, nothing more.

Theresienstadt was a transit camp where prisoners were held before being deported to the extermination centers. It was also designated as a destination for elderly German, Austrian, and Czech Jews, for those wounded during the Great War or decorated with the Iron Cross, and for prominent artists, musicians, and scientists whose disappearance would trigger questions. At Theresienstadt, according to Nazi fiction, Jews were well treated. The reality was that most of the elderly died of starvation or disease, and of the fifteen thousand children who passed through the camp, 90 percent were taken to the killing centers.

The deportations from Berlin started on October 18, 1941, almost a year before Bruno and Ella were taken. No one had come back. That first train carried Jews to Lodz, a city in central Poland, previously home to 160,000 Jews. After occupying Poland, the Nazis confined the Jews of Lodz into a ghetto and used them as forced labor to sew uniforms and manufacture electrical equipment for the military. The workers received food rations, rations so meager that thousands died from starvation.[3] That was the beginning of transports that eventually sent more than fifty-five thousand Jews from Berlin to various camps in the east.[4]

Thousands in Lodz were later driven out and brought to the killing center in Chelmno, thirty miles away. There the victims were killed in trucks as carbon monoxide from exhaust fumes was transmitted back to a sealed rear compartment. Tens of thousands never even arrived at the work camps. They were taken directly from the trains, marched out to the forests of Rumbula in Latvia, executed by gunfire, and thrown into massive graves.

As brutal and violent as these murders were, Hitler demanded a more comprehensive solution to the Jewish problem. This directive was orally relayed to Reichsmarschall Hermann Göring, who issued written orders to the chief security officer and head of the Gestapo, Reinhard Heydrich. The orders called for the implementation of a grand-scale plan, a systematic approach for "the Final Solution of the Jewish question."

On January 20, 1942, Heydrich invited fourteen senior government officials and high-ranking SS officers to a conference in Wannsee, a suburb of Berlin. The Wannsee Conference allowed Heydrich to consolidate power and bring these elite officers and government leaders together to coordinate mass murder. The men at the conference were well educated; seven held doctorate degrees and a few practiced law and served as judges. Despite their education, not one man challenged or even questioned the systematic murder of all Jews in Europe. The crimes of the Holocaust were developed and executed with precision by well-educated, evil men.

Heydrich and the other fourteen men understood Hitler's intentions long before the Wannsee Conference. It was Reinhard Heydrich who had supervised the death squads that followed the German army when they invaded the Soviet Union in June 1941. These mobile killing units, the Einsatzgruppen, shot and killed civilians. They entered small villages and forced political leaders, clergy, communists, Gypsies, and Jews to march out into the fields, where they were ruthlessly executed.

One of the officers who sat calmly at the conference table was Adolf Eichmann. When the war broke out, Eichmann arranged the train schedules for deporting Jews to overcrowded ghettos in Poland where starvation was rampant and typhus was widespread.

Eichmann came to Wannsee prepared with numbers. He had compiled lists of the Jewish population in every occupied country as well as countries at war with Germany. Immediately after the conference, Eichmann supervised large-scale deportations to the extermination centers at Belzec, Sobibor, Treblinka, and Auschwitz-Birkenau.

More than fifteen years after the end of World War II, Adolf Eichmann sat in a courtroom in Jerusalem charged with war crimes and crimes against humanity. The trial began in April 1961. I remember sitting in the living room with Mom as she watched the black-and-white broadcast of the Eichmann trial on television. I was ten years old.

"Why is he sitting in a glass box?" I asked.

"That's Eichmann. The people there, they hate him. Somebody might bring a gun and shoot him. Could happen," Mom answered.

Eichmann, wearing a dark suit, white shirt, and tie, sat in bulletproof enclosure to prevent an assassination attempt. He had escaped capture after the war and lived under the alias Ricardo Klement in Argentina. Mossad, the Israeli intelligence agency, located Eichmann, arrested him, and secretly brought him to Israel to stand trial.

"What do you mean, somebody might kill him? He's in a courtroom." I didn't understand the suffering and rage inside the Holocaust survivors sitting in the courtroom and the dozens who took the witness stand and told their stories.

"Courtroom, doesn't matter. What he did was so terrible. People want him dead," Mom replied, more interested in watching TV than answering my questions.

Eichmann, a slender man with a high forehead and thick glasses, repeatedly stated he was only following orders. He spoke in a calm tone, without dramatic gestures. As a child, I watched the trial on television, confused that this ordinary-looking man could have been so evil. As an adult, I returned to watch videos of the trial, angry at Eichmann's detachment. He spoke as an observer of events, with no remorse for his actions. His words no longer confused me. I saw him for his actions and his brutality that could not be hidden by a thin veneer of normal behavior.

Far more than Eichmann's testimony, I was moved by the words of the survivors who stood and spoke about parents severely beaten and children taken away from their mothers. They had witnessed evil, and their words impacted me greatly.

The court found him guilty of war crimes and crimes against humanity, concluding that "Eichmann had done everything in his power to interpret and implement the orders he received in as extreme and harsh a manner as possible."[5] He was sentenced to death, and on June 1, 1962, seventeen years after the war ended, Eichmann was executed by hanging.

* * *

When Lilo and Hans Martin walked to Klara's apartment after their parents were taken away, they entered a familiar place, a home they had visited often. Klara protected Lilo and Hans Martin with shelter, food, and affection, and kept curious neighbors away. But so much was out of her control.

In January and February of 1943, the Nazis stepped up their efforts to make Berlin *Judenfrei*. No longer satisfied with knocks on the door, the SS stopped people on the street and demanded to see their identification card. Anyone without proper papers was arrested and deported. A young man not in uniform was especially vulnerable. There was no official word, but on the day Hans ventured out of Klara's home and failed to return in the evening, Lilo knew.

When Mom tells me about her time at Klara's house, there is one day she always comes back to, one day that stands out. "People disappeared, it was a crazy time. People didn't come back, I knew what happened. He was caught, it happened so fast." Mom and her brother had been a unit of two, protecting and supporting each other. Losing her brother, her best friend, was a sharp cut inside the open wound of losing her parents.

Mom talks about her brother all the time, sometimes with deep longing but more often with a smile, remembering moments when they were kids. There are winter stories of skating on the frozen lakes and summer stories of swimming and biking and ice cream cones. And memories of Hans turning her brand-new baby carriage, a birthday present, upside down and riding it like a race car. I know these stories well, and they connect me to my uncle, a man I've never met.

* * *

Early in the war, the British Royal Air Force directed its attacks on military targets, not residential areas. As the war continued, the air raids expanded to strategic bombing with attacks on civilian areas within cities, especially in Hamburg and in Berlin. When Lilo was living in hiding with Klara, the high-pitched sirens were all too familiar.

In February 1943, after Hans had been taken, flying shrapnel and debris from a nearby explosion damaged Klara's building. Firefighters and police converged at the site and ordered all tenants to evacuate. Klara could no longer protect Lilo.

Now completely alone, Lilo walked towards the familiar streets of her old neighborhood. Her boyfriend, Ernst, was already in hiding with his parents. He had told her about the small room, about the German couple, but never the address. Once a week, on the day he walked the streets and bought food on the black market, he saw her. Lilo could depend on seeing Ernst on a specified day, at a predetermined place, but otherwise, there was no way to reach him.

She headed towards the ice cream store on Olivaer Platz. Before the war, it was a place where teenagers gathered, and it continued to be an informal meeting place where those who lived underground met briefly and exchanged information. One of Lilo's friends, Ernst Schwerin and his girlfriend, Ushi, were planning to cross the border into Switzerland. They had secured false identity cards, hoarded funds for food, trains, and bribes, reviewed road maps and train schedules, and procured handguns. They had asked Lilo to join them, a proposition she considered. At that time, Hans had already been arrested and Lilo was living by herself with Klara. She had discussed the idea with Ernst, but he was not at all interested. It was far too dangerous, too great a risk, plus he would never leave his parents. Perhaps if Hans were still here, Lilo thought, they could do this. But without him, it would be impossible.

As she continued walking, Lilo saw a familiar figure across the street. The woman was a bit taller than Lilo. She was thin, rather angular, and walked with a determined, purposeful step. Felice Schragenheim, a Jewish classmate, was someone safe to approach. Lilo hurried over and said, "Felice, do you remember me from the Bismarck Lyceum?"

"Lilo Jacoby. Of course I remember you. You were in the class behind me."

In the years when they had been in school, Felice had been living with her father, her stepmother Käthe, and her older sister Irene. Felice explained that her father had died of a heart attack, her sister was living in England, and her stepmother had gone to Palestine.

"I could have gone to Palestine with Käthe, but I was holding out for America."

Lilo listened, envious of the opportunities Felice lightly tossed about.

Felice paused, looked down the street, and with no one standing within earshot, she continued, "Uncle Walter lives in Chicago. He provided the paperwork and arranged passage on a ship. I had prepared clothes to bring, packed my trunk, but there were delays. Lilo, I was so close, almost on that ship, but then the diplomatic relations between Germany and the U.S. ended. No one could leave. I was trapped."

The two women continued their conversation as they walked on the side streets around the park. "For a while, I lived with Oma. Then in August, the Gestapo came for her. She was seventy-four, still so elegant. They took her and her brother, who was even older."

Whenever someone passed by, Felice fell silent. Once they were alone again, Felice continued, "Thinking that I will never see them again is unbearable. Perhaps in Theresienstadt they'll have a chance to survive."

Lilo nodded. That was how she felt about her parents, how she steadied herself from despair.

"Now, I'm living underground with my friend Inge Wolf. Her parents know I'm Jewish, but they let me stay."[6]

"Lilo, so I've told you my story. And you?"

When Lilo explained her situation, Felice gave her the address of a safe house. Felice and Inge were in a relationship, and they had a network of girlfriends living in various places.

When Lilo moved into the apartment where Felice had sent her, she entered a world that was different from anything she knew. The women were affectionate towards each other, and they tried to make Lilo feel welcome. But for Lilo it was strange and uncomfortable, and not a place she could stay. After a few days, she decided to leave, return to Olivaer Platz, and search for another hiding place. As Lilo walked out the door, Felice handed her a small bit of bread and passed on valuable information: "Be careful of Stella Goldschlag." Stella, a friend of Lilo and Felice, was working for the Gestapo as a catcher.

Catchers were Jews who bartered for their freedom by informing on other Jews. They walked the streets of Berlin looking for familiar faces, acquaintances or even friends, and pointed them out to the Gestapo standing nearby. Stella Goldschlag was one of the most notorious catchers. She was tall and slender, with wavy blond hair, sparkling blue eyes, and a flirtatious smile. Lilo had been at parties in Stella's home, where Stella's father, a composer, sat at the piano and played popular music. All the boys had a crush on her, and all the girls were jealous.

Stella had turned into an accomplice for the Gestapo after being arrested and brutally beaten. In return for identifying underground Jews, those in hiding, she was promised that neither she nor her parents would be deported.[7]

Once, alone on the street and looking for shelter, Lilo caught a glimpse of Stella standing with a small group of people in front of a café. Lilo turned down a side street, continued walking at a steady pace and breathed a sigh of relief at the absence of footsteps behind her.

Survival meant constant surveillance, carefully watching everyone without attracting attention. Walking on the street was a game of cat and mouse. Most of all, it was a horrible game of luck.

Lilo had nowhere to go. With no money for food and no place of shelter, she considered turning herself in to the authorities. She was terribly hungry and afraid of every shadow. It was impossible to imagine surviving on the street. *Just a few more days*, Lilo thought. *Hold on, just a few more days till you see Ernst again.*

Lilo spent two nights in the public bathroom of the Bahnhof Zoo railway station. To avoid being caught by the cleaning crew, she sat on the toilet with her legs tucked in tightly, hoping and praying no one would open the door. She could hear the cleaning lady running water in the sink and mopping down the floor, but she never opened the door to clean the toilet.

In the morning, when it was safe to come out, Lilo deliberately flushed the toilet, turned the door latch, and casually walked to the sink. She washed her hands and face, smoothed out her wrinkled clothes, and returned to the street. Appearing dirty or disheveled was a sign of living underground.

She divided the little remaining bread into four small pieces to last the day. While walking the street, she heard someone call out her name. Lilo started to run, fearing it was Stella. Again, she heard, "Lilo, please wait. Stop." She glanced back, startled to recognize Eva Cassirer.

How could she let Eva see her like this? Of all her classmates, Eva was the last person Lilo wanted to see. Ashamed and embarrassed of how she looked, she continued running. Eva called out again, "Lilo, please wait, don't be afraid."

Not knowing where to run, Lilo stopped, stood still, and allowed Eva to approach.

"Do you have somewhere to stay?" Eva asked.

Lilo shook her head.

"Mutti needs help in the house. You know the house is so big and we have no one for cleaning or cooking." Eva reached into her bag for a scrap of paper, scribbled down her address, and handed that over along with some money, enough for bus fare.

"Come over in the evening, after it's dark. Perhaps Mutti can help."

6

HIDING

Lilo stared out the window as the bus left the familiar apartment buildings around the Ku'damm and headed west toward Eva's home in Grunewald, the section of Berlin with stately mansions and a forest with thousands of acres of pine, spruce, and birch trees. Grunewald was only a bus ride from the city's center but to Lilo, it felt far from the deportation center on Grosse Hamburger Strasse. She tried to remember childhood times of hiking along the lakes and canals of the forest, memories that were quickly fading. Lilo took out the crumpled piece of paper from her coat pocket – Wildpfad 28.

Lilo knew Eva from her school days at the Bismarck Lyceum. They were never close friends, but Lilo trusted her. Eva, the girl who came to school in a chauffeur-driven car, had a Jewish background. Lilo did not fear betrayal.

She stepped off the bus and walked onto unfamiliar streets. It was a neighborhood of villas, and each house was far apart from its neighbors and recessed away from the road. Nothing at all like Klara's apartment where people could spy on you from their kitchen window. A five-foot-high black metal fence stretched along the property line of Wildpfad 28. The house in the distance was dark, except for a single light. Lilo followed the long stone walkway up to the heavy wooden front door, took in a deep breath, smoothed out her coat, and knocked on the door. Eva's mother, Hannah Sotscheck, appeared at the first knock and brought Lilo into a spacious and airy kitchen. Large black and white tiles covered the floor, and a row of light blue cabinets stood along the side wall. Eva was standing in the kitchen and offered Lilo a small, reassuring smile. Lilo looked at the few slices of bread and bit of jam set out on the table. She could have easily devoured everything in sight. But she limited herself to one slice of bread and jam, her need to make a good impression overpowering her hunger pangs. Lilo knew manners in this house were extremely important, and she understood that the first priority was to please Mrs. Sotscheck.

Mrs. Sotscheck looked directly at Lilo and said, "Eva tells me your parents and brother were deported."

"Yes, some time ago for my parents." Lilo stopped, not wanting to say more. After a few moments, she added, "But for my brother, I don't know."

The three women sat in silence.

"I fear he's been taken," Lilo said. Mrs. Sotscheck asked no other questions.

Before the war, Hannah Sotscheck had a staff of servants to run the house and care for the property. Now there was only a gardener. Mrs. Sotscheck needed a maid to help in the kitchen and take care of whatever else she deemed necessary. Lilo listened, grateful for a place to stay, but she wondered why this wealthy woman would take such a risk to herself and her daughter, just to have a maid. Lilo pushed those thoughts away and headed down to a bed in the basement.

* * *

The three-story villa was filled with treasures. Hand-knotted Persian rugs with deep wool pile in shades of dark red and ivory lay on the floor. The shelves in the library were overflowing with novels and plays by Johann Goethe and Friedrich Schiller. The house itself was commissioned by Leo Blumenreich, Mrs. Sotscheck's second husband, as a replica of Goethe's garden house, and Blumenreich, an art dealer, decorated the home with original paintings and drawings.

Mrs. Sotscheck, a woman in her mid-fifties, had married well, two times. She was tall and slim-waisted, with fine, honey-blond hair. Her home in Grunewald was a far cry from the farm outside of Berlin where she grew up and learned to care for animals and handle household chores. Her family was Christian, but religion did not play a role in her adult life nor in the lives of her two Jewish husbands.

Her first husband, Alfred Cassirer, was Eva's father. The youngest of six children, Alfred was born into a family prominent in academics, the arts, and industry. Alfred and his brother Hugo owned and operated Dr. Cassirer & Co., a factory that manufactured rubber-coated wires. The business became quite profitable as a major international supplier in the electronics industry before World War II.[1]

In 1923, three years after their only child, Eva, was born, Alfred and Hannah divorced. Eva stayed with her mother yet maintained a close relationship with her father, along with her mother's new husband, Blumenreich. In a sad turn of events, both men died of natural causes in 1932, and Eva lost the love of two fathers.

* * *

Soon after Lilo arrived, a German naval officer, Herr Kutcher, moved in. During the war, the government relied on *Einquartierung*, a system comparable to quartering or billeting, where soldiers were housed in private homes. Herr Kutcher loved tennis and spent most of his free time at the Rot-Weiss (red-white) tennis club. He would return to the house in the late afternoon stylishly dressed in white shorts, white shirt, and a navy-blue blazer with shiny gold buttons. He was very polite but curious about the young woman who worked in the house. He asked many questions. Perhaps he suspected something or perhaps he just found the maid attractive. Lilo was nineteen, and she enjoyed their brief conversations. In normal times, she would have liked to go out with him. But Mrs. Sotscheck demanded she stay away, and after a few weeks, he left much to Lilo's relief, touched with a bit of disappointment.

Lilo was living openly in the house as a maid, but under a new name and identity. Eva had secured false papers, and Lilo was now Liselotte Lehmann, an art student at the university. Most often, girls who worked as maids came from families outside Berlin. They were usually not well educated and spoke in regional dialects. As Lilo spoke *Hochdeutsch*, standard German, with correct grammar, there needed to be a reason behind her situation as a maid. Eva created a workable background story. Liselotte had suffered a terrible tragedy. Her parents had been killed in an automobile accident, and now, dear Liselotte had to work to help pay expenses at the university. This alias was a good match for Lilo, as long as no one probed too deeply with questions about artists or art history.

To minimize suspicion, Mrs. Sotscheck expanded the story to say that Liselotte had her own apartment. She did not sleep in the house and only came for a few hours to clean. Each evening the maid politely said *Gute Nacht* to any visitor. Many people came in and out of the house, some for a brief evening visit; others stayed for days and even months. Lilo walked out the door with a flashlight and directed the light beam towards a spot about 50 feet away from the front door. There, hidden below the grass, was a flat metal grate that covered the entrance to the *Luftschutzkeller*, the underground shelter. Lilo climbed down a few rough steps into a narrow space and waited. There were muffled sounds all around. Lilo listened, trying to separate the noise of squirrels running through leaves and branches from footsteps of soldiers patrolling the streets. After some time, Lilo climbed out and looked back at the house. When the guests had left and everyone had gone off to bed, Eva opened the shutters in the third-floor bedroom window. That was the signal it was safe to come back inside. If the shutters were closed, Lilo returned to the bunker and waited. She prayed no one witnessed her climbing in or out. The long hours in a small, cold hole were terrible, but the nights when the British Royal Air Force bombers flew overhead were even worse.

Lilo's days in the house were filled with routine household chores of dusting and vacuuming. It was hard not to stop and stare at the original artwork created by masters. She gently dusted the frames around the Max Liebermann paintings, the drawings by Rembrandt and Rubens, and carefully wiped the sculptures on shelves and bookcases throughout the library. One day Lilo failed to notice a vacuum cleaner cord wrapped around the leg of an end table. As she maneuvered around the sofa, the cord pulled down the table holding an antique Chinese vase. Lilo watched in dismay as the vase fell and shattered. She picked up the shards of porcelain covering the floor and feared the worst. To her surprise, Mrs. Sotscheck accepted the broken vase without anger. She reprimanded Lilo for her carelessness, but the incident was soon forgotten.

Lilo worked diligently, not just to polish the parquet floors but to find ways to please Mrs. Sotscheck. She cleaned and shined the shoes and boots, repaired torn hems, sewed loose buttons on jackets before they fell off, and served tea at any time of day or night.

Each morning Lilo formally greeted Mrs. Sotscheck, saying, *Guten Morgen gnädige Frau. Haben Sie gut geschlafen?* Good morning my dear lady. Did you sleep well? *Gnädige Frau* was a bit over-the-top. It was extremely formal and old-fashioned.

One morning after breakfast Mrs. Sotscheck remarked, "I wish I could tell your mother how nice she brought you up. Someday, I hope I will. You have nice manners, you are respectful."

These words stayed with Mom for decades. She has repeated this story to me so often to remind me of the importance of good manners. I hold back from disagreeing, from trying to explain that today's world is different.

For Mom, good manners brought security and affection. I was given both, even when I became impatient hearing Mom tell and retell her stories of life in Berlin and when I became frustrated with her English grammar mistakes that I tried to correct. I grew up in a peaceful time with parents who loved and protected me. How can I judge my mother's views on manners? So I just listen patiently to stories I've heard before.

* * *

When Lilo came into the house, she told Mrs. Sotscheck about Ernst, her boyfriend, who was living in hiding.

"Lilo, promise me you will never tell Ernst or anyone where you live," Mrs. Sotscheck said sternly and then added, "If you break this promise, I will not keep you."

Lilo agreed, but silently knew the promise would be broken. She trusted Ernst completely. He would never betray her, never reveal any names or places, even if captured. But Lilo could not say those words; she would never disagree with Mrs. Sotscheck. Ernst always knew where Lilo lived, first in Klara's apartment and now in this mansion in Grunewald. But Ernst kept the address of where he and his parents were hiding a secret; and Lilo never asked.

* * *

When I began writing, I was troubled by Dad's decision to keep this information hidden from Mom. What if the house on Wildpfad 28 was bombed? What if Mom had nowhere to go and needed to reach him?

As I continued to research and write their story, I realized my thoughts belonged in normal days, in peaceful times, not in the world of Berlin in 1943. I imagined Dad was reassured knowing Mom was protected by a wealthy family, by people who gave her food, shelter, and false identity papers. His life was completely different. No one had false papers, no one had enough to eat, and three people were confined to one small room. Dad needed to protect his parents and himself and the people who sheltered them. He needed to keep his hiding place a secret.

* * *

On the days that Ernst ventured out to black-market vendors in Alexanderplatz, he found a way to see Lilo. These vendors provided many Germans, including Hannah Sotscheck, a way to supplement the meager ration cards. The government-issued cards allowed a person less than half a pound of meat per week, but with money, everything was available. Mrs. Sotscheck paid the high price demanded for items such as coffee and sugar. She bought fruits, vegetables, and poultry from friends with farms outside Berlin. Food was a social necessity. It allowed her to host dinner parties for diplomats and military officials and maintain good relations with men in power.

At these events, Mrs. Sotscheck ordered Lilo to avoid conversation and remain in the kitchen as much as possible. Yet at one party, a Bulgarian gentleman noticed this pretty maid, and as she served dinner, he asked her name. "Liselotte," she replied and quickly walked away. When she came back with dessert, he asked more questions about her home and family.

As she cleared the plates off the table, he said, "I don't want to know any more about you, but I think you're wasting your time here. You shouldn't be a maid."[2]

Lilo steadied the tray of dishes and continued back to the kitchen, ignoring his words. He followed her and added, "Come with me. I'll help you. I can do more for you, and I promise, I won't ask any questions."

Lilo placed the heavy tray down on the kitchen table, not trusting herself to keep the plates from crashing. She thanked him politely, simply saying how happy she was in her current position. A sink full of dirty dishes kept her occupied in the kitchen. When the dining room became silent, and the guests left after finishing their after-dinner drinks, Lilo told Mrs. Sotscheck of the conversation. Mrs. Sotscheck said nothing and offered no additional information about the guest. No further inquiries were made by the Bulgarian gentleman, and no other dinner invitations were ever issued to him.

* * *

In all my conversations with Mom about her life in hiding, I never heard about any precautions taken to protect Eva from arrest. This might seem surprising given Eva was a Mischling first degree, a half Jew. I believe the reason rests with the somewhat arbitrary Nazi policy towards Mischlinge and "privileged" Jews, those married to non-Jews. Some were sent to labor camps, not death camps, and many were never deported. Before the war, intermarriage was common. The Nazis expected Aryans to turn a blind eye when their Jewish neighbors were deported, but would Aryan Omas and Opas be as complacent if their own grandchildren were taken?

The Rosenstrasse Protest is an example of non-Jews protecting their Jewish spouses. In late February 1943, 1,800 men were arrested and taken to a holding center on 2-4 Rosenstrasse, in the heart of Berlin. The men were either Jews married to Aryan women or half Jews, Mischlinge. When their husbands and sons failed to return home from work, the women gathered in the street and chanted, *"Gebt uns unsere Männer wieder!"* Give us our husbands back![3] The women, wives and mothers, were ordered to move away; they were threatened with machine guns, but no shots were fired. After a week of daily protests, the government began releasing the men. All were eventually sent home. Even the twenty-five who had been deported to Auschwitz were returned to Berlin. This situation was rare. Indeed it was the only mass public demonstration in Nazi Germany against the deportation of Jews. Yet it reflects a gray area, an undefined space where German Jews and non-Jews intersected, and a moment when the Nazi hierarchy acted in a most unpredictable way.

There is a troubling question that remains unanswered. Why did Hannah Sotscheck protect my mother? This is something I struggle to understand, and the only answer my mother provides is, "She needed someone to clean the house." This gives me no satisfaction.

All I can offer is that Mrs. Sotscheck was a wealthy woman, skillful in using her resources to provide an open home where Nazis frequently gathered. Perhaps there was an element of friendship that dissuaded officers from asking too many questions, or perhaps there were bribes, gifts discreetly given to protect those living in the house. Mrs. Sotscheck's thoughts remain a mystery, but her actions speak most clearly. Twice she defied cultural pressures of antisemitism and married Jewish men. Eva was part of a Jewish family, the Cassirers, and perhaps Hannah Sotscheck wanted to shelter a Jewish woman, as an act of compassion and solidarity, not that dissimilar to the women marching in protest on Rosenstrasse.

* * *

Hiding in the open and pretending to be someone else was not the only danger Lilo faced. In 1943, the Allies began an aggressive aerial campaign, bombing cities in central Germany, on the outskirts of Nuremberg, then advancing north to Hamburg. By autumn, the Allies focused their efforts on Berlin.

This was a policy change from the previous strategy of precision bombing, where attacks were limited to military and industrial sites and civilians were not the intended target. While thousands of civilians were killed in precision bombing raids, their death was collateral damage, the byproduct of inaccurate bombing. The shift in strategy directed bombs to urban areas. The intent was to target Germany's labor force, create massive homelessness, and shatter morale.[4]

In one such attack in 1943, a bomb landed near Roseneck, a neighborhood of small grocery shops and cafés less than a half mile from Wildpfad 28. Lilo was riding her bike on an errand for Mrs. Sotscheck, a trip she had taken many times. She was pedaling past familiar stores when the sirens began blasting. There was a public underground shelter nearby, a few blocks away. Lilo had false papers, and maybe they would pass the test if examined. Not wanting to take the risk and with little time left, Lilo threw the bike aside, took cover under the trees, and crouched on the ground.

When the explosions stopped and the air thick with smoke, dirt, and sand cleared, Lilo looked out onto the silent street. There were gaping holes in buildings where windows once were and even larger holes where sections of wall were totally destroyed, leaving bedrooms and kitchens exposed. Her ears were still ringing from the noise of the explosion as she walked through broken bricks and found her bike, undamaged by tree branches lying all around. There was an old man lying dead in the middle of the street. He was a familiar figure, and before the explosion, he had nodded hello as she rode past him. Unhurt but badly shaken, Lilo picked up her bike and pedaled away.

The Allies' bombing of Berlin left thousands dead and hundreds of thousands homeless. Just as the government called upon private citizens to house soldiers, the government also required those with extra beds to provide shelter for those in need. Many strangers came into Mrs. Sotscheck's house for a few nights, sometimes longer. Lilo avoided them all, except for one.

Gerdi Asbach was an artist living in a rooftop studio apartment. When the Allies bombed Gerdi's home, they also destroyed the hiding place for her Jewish boyfriend. Mrs. Sotscheck shared this with Lilo when Gerdi arrived.

Gerdi was a tall, angular woman in her mid-forties, a woman with an enormous heart who looked at life with humor and regarded everyday problems as trivial. When Gerdi moved in, Lilo gained a friend and a confidante. At the end of the day when the kitchen floor was mopped for the last time, Lilo would sit in a small upstairs bedroom with Gerdi and speak openly about her parents, her brother, and Ernst. For Lilo, that magical spark, be it chemistry or love, was missing. Perhaps she would end the relationship after the war, but not now. These thoughts she shared with Gerdi, no one else.

On the days when Lilo had time for herself, she sometimes went back to see her old nanny, Klara Paschke. On one such visit, Lilo knocked on the door and Klara greeted her with a broad smile, waving a piece of newspaper in her hand.

"Lilo, Lilo, look what came in the mail!" Klara handed her the small slip of paper with a handwritten message. Lilo read the note, then read it again and again. She looked up at Klara in disbelief and shouted, "He's alive, Klara, he's alive." The two women hugged each other and jumped up and down as two young schoolgirls. They cried and wiped away tears blinding their eyes.

They stopped, examined the scrap of paper, and read the few words again. Hans Martin had done the impossible. He had made friends with a Nazi solider in Auschwitz. He found a soldier who mailed a note to Klara asking her to please send food. Unbelievable. The weight of weariness and fear lifted and lightness and color came back into Lilo's world.

Lilo shared this news with Mrs. Sotscheck, and the two women immediately gathered some bread along with a few cans of potatoes and a can of meat to send off to this soldier, an angel. A few weeks later, Hans sent a second note. The package had arrived. Was it possible to send another?

That was the last note, but those two messages were a miracle and enough to keep Lilo's hope alive.

Many visitors came into the house, and Lilo avoided contact if possible. But there was one guest who could be trusted. Dr. Hans Paret, a tall, trim, fair-haired, middle-aged gentleman, came once a week in the afternoon and shared coffee and cake with Mrs. Sotscheck. In autumn, when dark purple Italian plums were available, Lilo prepared *Pflaumenkuchen*, plum cake. If plums weren't available, blueberries or peaches would do, but plums were the best. This polite gentleman was Eva's financial guardian. He acknowledged Lilo with a courteous smile, but never posed questions or probed for information. Mrs. Sotscheck assured her not to worry.

Alfred Cassirer had selected Paret to manage his daughter's inheritance, which he had faithfully done since Alfred died in 1932. Paret was an interesting choice as he was not born into the family, and he was not Jewish. His connection came through marriage to Eva's cousin Suzanne. Selecting Paret proved to be a prescient decision as this German gentleman was in a far better position to protect Eva's inheritance than a Jewish relative who would have had his bank account monitored or confiscated by the Nazis.

While Gerdi Asbach and Hans Paret were people Lilo could trust, they were the exception. By and large, Lilo stayed away from visitors and neighbors and especially from General Friedrich Olbricht, who lived at Wildpfad 24, two doors away.[5] Mrs. Sotscheck had no direct contact with General Olbricht, but as he was the chief of the General Army Office, there was enough reason to keep distant.

On July 21, 1944, Mrs. Sotscheck sat at the breakfast table and spilled her cup of tea as she read the morning paper. She called out to Lilo and pointed to the article on the front page. There had been an assassination attempt on the life of the Führer, and General Olbricht was one of the chief architects of the mission, known as Operation Valkyrie. The plot was part of an attempted military coup to overthrow Hitler and take down the Nazi regime. The newspaper reported that a young officer, Colonel Claus von Stauffenberg, carried a bomb hidden in his briefcase into military headquarters where Hitler and twenty other officers convened for a strategy briefing. Stauffenberg positioned his briefcase under the table by Hitler's chair. When Stauffenberg exited the room to answer a pre-arranged phone call, the bomb exploded. Four men were killed, but Hitler was only slightly wounded. Olbricht and Stauffenberg were quickly arrested and executed.

Mrs. Sotscheck passed the newspaper to Lilo, and the two women looked at each other in disbelief and disappointment. All this time, Mrs. Sotscheck had carefully avoided contact with General Olbricht, never suspecting he would have orchestrated a coup d'état to remove Hitler from power.

Mrs. Sotscheck and Lilo shared disappointment over the failed assassination attempt, but to any outside visitor, they hid any trace of disloyalty to the Führer. *Who do you fear? Who do you trust? How do you know?*

* * *

February 1945: The temperature had been below the freezing point for most of the month. Snow spread over debris from bombed-out buildings, and icicles hung on bare tree limbs and street signs. Church steeples that once stood proud were stunted pillars with ragged edges. Great Britain and the U.S. had escalated the air war, and Berlin lay in ruins.

Lilo walked through the city streets on a sunless day, near the U-Bahn station on Potsdamer Strasse, expecting to see Ernst. It was a day they had planned to meet, and Ernst was always on time. Lilo waited five minutes, then walked down to the next corner, around the block to keep warm and to avoid attracting attention. She checked her watch again. He was twelve minutes late. Something was wrong. She knew all too well the possible reasons—he needed to change his course, too many Nazi soldiers on the street, too great a risk of being stopped and questioned. Perhaps there was a problem with his parents. Betty, Ernst's mother, was growing weaker, experiencing frequent dizzy spells and severe headaches. They had been hiding in that tiny room, with a lack of food and fresh air, for more than two years. Maybe Ernst couldn't leave, and perhaps, perhaps his luck had simply run out. Finally, Lilo left without an answer.

A few days later, Ernst called the house and asked to speak with Gerdi. He knew he could trust Gerdi and without offering any explanation, he simply left a message that he would meet Lilo next week, same place as before.

The following week, Lilo found Ernst already there, walking slowly back and forth, waiting for her. He looked terrible, paler than usual, eyes downcast. He was hunched over, staring at the ground. He found it difficult to speak. After a long period of silence, he said that his father died last week from a heart attack.

Lilo wasn't surprised. She had known Ernst for four years and often heard him speak about his father's medical problems. Lilo looked at Ernst, worried how he would handle this loss.

"There was no way to get him to a doctor, no way to get medicine, impossible to go to a hospital." Ernst repeated those words over and over, as though he couldn't escape the burden of his inability to save his father. "Even if by some miracle, I found a doctor willing to come to the house, the risk to Pissarius, the risk to my mother was too great."

Ernst stood next to Lilo for a long time, saying nothing. He looked at all the crushed stones and broken glass lying on the ground, and finally said, "We couldn't leave him in the apartment." Again there was silence. "We needed to move the body."

When nightfall came, Ernst had carefully wrapped his father in a quilted blanket. He had already emptied his father's trouser pockets of any papers that hinted of his identity. Pissarius helped Ernst lift the body onto a cart, and the two men headed towards the river. The Spree River was just a block from the apartment on Eisenbahnstrasse, a short distance. They walked silently, afraid of being stopped and questioned. Shadows from the streetlamps cut across the road and fell on snow piles by the building. It was silent, no noise from cars or buses, only a rhythmic squeak from the back wheel of the cart. When they reached the bridge, they pulled the cart up the steps, and Ernst gently picked up his father and lowered him into the cold, dark water. The two men quickly returned home. No one stopped them. Inside the small room, Betty was sitting in a chair, weeping. Ernst knelt down beside her, and they held each other through the night. The room that had protected three people now loomed strangely large.

Lilo hugged Ernst tightly, wept with him, but could find no words to take away the pain of grief and guilt.

* * *

Sixty-six years later I retraced the steps my father took to the river. I was there in December 2011, with my husband, Lenny, and my mother. It was a day of nasty weather, with morning snow turning to rain and by the evening, wet snow covered the sidewalks.

The three of us walked silently from Eisenbahnstrasse 15 to the river. The Brommy Bridge was destroyed in the war and had not been rebuilt. Our small funeral procession headed to the water without a casket or a body, but with the weight of memories. I pulled my coat in tight, kept my hands deep in my pockets, and stood on a small pier against a metal fence. This was as close as I could come to the past. I stared down into the dark water and tried to imagine my father's pain.

The river was a cemetery without headstones, without a place I could leave a stone.

* * *

In February 1945, when Leopold Joseph died, the war was not going well for Germany. The Allied troops that stormed the beaches of Normandy and liberated Paris were steadily moving towards the Rhine River. By March, Germany was being attacked on both the western and eastern fronts as the Red Army advanced across Poland and defeated the German forces in Hungary. By mid-April, they had surrounded Berlin. The Russians were consumed with rage and hatred over the millions of their comrades murdered by the Germans. Seizing Berlin was their prize, their revenge for the soldiers killed in Moscow and Stalingrad and the civilians who died from starvation during the blockade of Leningrad. The Russian soldiers drove their tanks and rode their horses through the residential neighborhoods of Berlin, even the high-end streets of Grunewald. They threw grenades, set off explosives, and forced their way into homes, demanding food, liquor, money, jewelry, and women, whatever they wanted.

In the far back corner of the basement in Wildpfad 28, Lilo huddled close to Eva and Frau Riebensahm, and heard the men on horseback break through the front door. Gerdi Asbach had since moved out, and her bed was now occupied by Gerda Riebensahm, a pianist in her mid-forties. The three women hid together behind a partition of furniture and boxes stacked floor to ceiling. Lilo heard the horses' hoofs on the parquet wooden floor above her head and the heavy boots of men stomping up the stairs. They rushed through the bedrooms shouting, *Frauen! Frauen!* Mrs. Sotscheck offered no protest and stood silent as the horses trampled on chairs, ripped the sofas, and knocked down tables. She had covered her hair with a scarf, applied makeup to darken wrinkles, walked slowly and hunched over to create the appearance of a frail old lady. She had selected pieces of old jewelry to wear, rings, a watch, and bracelets, nothing of value.

The original paintings had been removed, stored in the basement, and replaced with inexpensive artwork.

Mrs. Sotscheck set out bottles of liquor and gave away one ring and then another and another, and with the few Russian words she knew, she said, "No women, nobody here, just an old lady."

The three women in the basement heard everything. They sat in silence, terrified, waiting to hear the tread of heavy boots descending. It never happened. For hours they sat still, afraid to move or make a sound that would attract attention.

In the evening, when the soldiers were gone, Mrs. Sotscheck brought the women food, water, and buckets for a toilet, but she did not allow them to return upstairs. "Not yet," she warned. "It's not safe."

The next morning the Russians returned, as Mrs. Sotscheck feared they would. But this time they brought bread, butter, and marmalade for the kind old lady.

On May 7, 1945, less than three weeks after the Russians seized Berlin, Germany unconditionally surrendered. The following day, the Allies celebrated VE day with huge cheering crowds in Buckingham Palace and Times Square. There was silence in Berlin. There was relief that the fighting had ended, grief over the death of so many young soldiers, despair over a city destroyed, and profound uncertainty about the future.

When the war ended, the gardener and Lilo recognized each other as Jews. During the war years, they hardly spoke to one another. But now, this older gentleman who quietly tended the bushes and plants around the house approached Lilo and said, "I always knew." Lilo smiled and replied, "So did I."

The question of what happened to her family was foremost in Lilo's mind. In her heart, she knew her parents were not coming back. But maybe, just maybe, her brother was still alive. The war was over, but for Lilo, there was no celebration.

For Betty the end of the war meant leaving the small room on Eisenbahnstrasse. Betty had been in that space for 27 months. She had lived through days and nights of listening to the high-pitched sound of bombers coming in and explosives landing outside. She had waited and worried endless hours for Ernst, and she had lived through the death of her husband. Now the war was over. With nerves frayed, Betty held on to her son's arm and tentatively walked outside, not trusting she was safe. Ernst brought his mother back to the apartment and returned to the street by himself.

Blocks away Russian soldiers were patrolling the area, looking for Nazis. As Ernst came around the corner, a Russian aimed his rifle at Ernst and ordered him to halt. The solider saw a young, thin man with straight blond hair and bright blue eyes, a man who resembled so many Nazis.

Trembling, Ernst shouted, *"Jude, Jude! Ich bin Jude!"*

The soldier understood that much German, but shook his head and kept the rifle pointed at Ernst. "Recite the Sh'ma," the Russian demanded. The words came quickly, and Ernst shouted out, *"Sh'ma Yisroel adonoy elohenu adonoy echod."* Hear O Israel, the Lord our God, the Lord is One.

The soldier removed his finger from the trigger, lowered the gun, and his face broke into a warm smile. He ran over to Ernst, embraced him, and said, "I am also a Jew."[6] The world had turned upside down.

* * *

My parents lived in Germany through a time of tremendous upheaval. In 1933, the year Hitler came to power, there were 160,000 Jews in Berlin. Restrictions and persecution began immediately. Jews were no longer welcomed in schools, in jobs, or on park benches. Hitler's massive rallies in Nuremberg with young boys carrying flags and wearing swastika armbands convinced many to emigrate. By 1941, Berlin's Jewish population had fallen to 65,000. After October of that year, Jews could no longer leave. The Joseph family was trapped by restrictive U.S. immigration quotas, and Bruno Jacoby still believed Hitler's time in office would soon end.

That was when the trains began running east. In total, 50,500 Jews from Berlin were deported. Only 1,600 returned.[7]

My mother and father lived underground in Berlin in completely different situations. They both attributed their survival to luck, incredible good fortune. That indeed is true. While their distinct and dissimilar personalities shaped their stories, I believe it was luck, encounters with honorable people at crucial moments, and a divine spirit that saved them.

In May 1945, when the war was over and the noise of exploding grenades was replaced by bicycle horns and mothers pushing strollers, a scattering of people emerged from hiding. It is estimated that 7,000 Jews had gone underground in Berlin. Most died from bombs, disease, or betrayal. Yet a handful, about 1,400, survived.[8] Against long odds, three of those who emerged were Betty, Ernst, and Lilo.

Eva Cassirer

Hannah Sotscheck

Wildpfad 28, Berlin

Leopold Joseph

7

THE WAR IS OVER

The long-awaited victory of the Allied forces stopped the bombs, ended the deportation to the camps, and opened the gates of the death factories. Berlin, the focus of hundreds of Allied air attacks, was destroyed. The rubble in the streets from falling bricks and the broken windows reflected a defeated city and a city in mourning.

The time in hiding had left Betty physically weak. She had lost weight and her eyesight had deteriorated. She ventured out a bit by herself, but mostly with her son.

For Ernst, the immediate question was where to live. Ernst made his way back to his old neighborhood and the apartment on Linienstrasse 5. He stepped around scraps of metal piled high on the sidewalks. Smoke and dust hung in the air, broken cars lined the streets, and only a few buses were running. His house no longer existed.

From where the house once was, Ernst walked toward the Central Market Hall where he and his father along with hundreds of other merchants once made a living. Not one block in this area stood undamaged, and the market hall itself, while still standing, was ruined.

When the war ended, the Allies divided Berlin into four zones, separately controlled by the United States, Russia, Great Britain, and France. Ernst found a furnished apartment on 12 Fredericiastrasse, the British sector. It was a comfortable place with plenty of room, even for Lilo if she chose to move in.

Lilo had not heard a word from her parents since she received that one postcard stamped from Theresienstadt. She held little hope of seeing them again. Bruno and Ella Jacoby were 63 and 54 when they were deported. The survivors who slowly returned were young men and women.

In the summer of 1945, Lilo held on tightly to memories of pre-war days. She thought about walking arm-in-arm with her father past the elegant shops on Kurfürstendamm. They would look at the mannequins in the window wearing elegant silk blouses and cream-colored linen jackets. Such clothes were expensive, but as Lilo reasoned, it didn't hurt to look. Lilo remembered her father reading his newspaper and heard his voice as he laughed with friends over a card game of Skat. She could smell the cigar smoke mingled with the aroma of beef rouladen simmering on the stove. She remembered celebrating her mother's birthday with flowers and poems. Lilacs were her favorite. There was always a poem to read, a poem written by her father.

Lilo was struggling with the question of where to live and how to create a future. For so long she had thought only of the current day. *Be careful where you walk. Be careful what you say. No, this person cannot be trusted.* Now, when it was time to move forward, putting the broken pieces back together was overwhelming.

As Lilo considered the next step, Mrs. Sotscheck said, "My dear child, I know you are praying that your parents or your brother will return. I want the same for you. But what if they don't?"

No answer.

Mrs. Sotscheck continued, "If no one comes back, stay here with Eva and me. You don't need to be alone. I can help you return to school, pay for your education."

These words brought tears to Lilo's eyes. She held Mrs. Sotscheck in the highest esteem and adored this woman who protected her. Mrs. Sotscheck had played a shrewd game with the Nazis, opening her home to soldiers, protecting her daughter, and hiding the Jewish identity of her maid and gardener.

Lilo thought over Mrs. Sotscheck's words. Staying in the house meant security. It meant an opportunity to finish school. She understood her work as a maid would be over. Yet . . . it was far more complicated. It would be difficult, if not impossible, to remain in the house without being the servant. She would always feel indebted, and there would be an unspoken obligation to please Mrs. Sotscheck.

Lilo wanted to be free, free from the house with priceless antiques and expectations of how to behave. That was clear, but questions of where to live and how to support herself were far more difficult.

In the end, Lilo decided to move into the apartment with Ernst and Betty.

* * *

It is sad for me to write that my mother didn't move into the apartment because she loved my father. Mom always said, "If my brother had come back, I wouldn't have moved in with your father. But in those days I had no idea what had happened to him. And here was Ernst—he was strong and someone who would take care of me. I was afraid to make a life by myself. I knew he was a good person, and I knew he loved me. He always loved me more than I loved him. And I thought, 'What is love?' After the war, I saw love from a different point of view."

My mother was not the first young woman to stay with a man for reasons other than love. Whatever affection existed at one time gradually faded, and their marriage as I knew it unraveled into a troubled relationship without love.

* * *

Among the survivors who came back as the weeks went by was Lilo's close childhood friend Lucy (Lux) Emmerich. Lux had survived horrible medical experiments in Auschwitz, but spoke little about what she endured, except to say she would never be able to have children. Lux later traveled to America and married a distant relative, thirty years older and very wealthy. Some may have wondered why a charming young woman married such an old man, but to Lux it made perfect sense.

A few months later someone knocked on the door of the apartment where Lilo was living with Ernst and Betty. She opened the door with hesitation, saw a man she didn't recognize and then heard a voice long forgotten: "Lilo, don't you know who I am? Don't you remember? It's me, Hans Peter."

Lilo pulled together a fuzzy memory. Hans Peter Messerschmidt was a close friend of her brother and a boy she once liked, so many years ago. He was tall, almost a head above her. As a teenager, he would humor her by walking beside her in the street so she could gain an inch or more on the sidewalk.

"How did you find me? How did you know where I live?" she asked.

"On the board at Grosse Hamburger Strasse," he replied. The old-age home, the place where thousands had been deported, served as a central location spot for survivors to reconnect.

In March 1943, Hans Peter was deported to Auschwitz and was there for almost two years. As the Soviets approached the camp in January 1945, the guards ordered him and the other prisoners to march to a smaller camp, Gleiwitz. From there, the Nazis transferred him to Buchenwald. When the war ended, when the camps were liberated, he was too weak to return home. With medical attention, nourishment, and rest, he regained strength and made his way back to Berlin.[1]

But Hans Peter hadn't come to tell Lilo his story. He had good news, he told her—wonderful news. "Hans Martin is alive," he said. "We were together at Auschwitz and at liberation. He's coming home."

Lilo stood shaking, listening to words she had only dreamed about.

Lilo hugged him tightly. To see Hans Peter standing there was nothing short of a miracle. He told her about time in the camps, how her brother told funny stories, did impressions of Hitler, and made everyone laugh.

She asked him to say the words again: "Your brother is alive. Hans Martin is coming home." Sunlight filled the room as Lilo repeated the words over and over again.

Weeks went by and Lilo waited for Hans Martin to return. She went down to the central location center to search for answers. Survivors had come back from Auschwitz, and many repeated the same narrative. "There were a few paths out of the camps. We divided into groups, about five in each. Our group made it out OK, but we never saw the others." More survivors returned with similar stories. Some knew a bit more. "There were Nazis patrolling areas outside the camp. The war was over, but they still had their handguns and ammunition."

No official information was available. No lists were distributed of who died. Weeks, months, and years went by, and Lilo continued to wait. Hans Martin continued to exist in her heart as a young, strong man of 21. Her eyes would shine and sparkle with stories of wonderful times they shared together in Berlin, before the war, before Hitler.

In my mother's world in Nazi Germany everything was a secret. People disappeared, and no one knew what happened. Even after the war, my mother never received any notification about her family. Neither her parents nor her brother ever returned, and that was the answer.

It took years for boxes of German records to be sorted, reviewed, and categorized. There were millions of documents with information on transports, lists of names along with dates and place of birth. There were reports by SS officers about the assets confiscated on the transports. And there were lists of numbers tattooed on the left arm of the prisoners. The elderly and the frail were never issued a number. They were taken off the train and immediately murdered.

In 1992 we found answers to many of our family's questions. That was the year I went to Israel along with my husband, children, and mother. My daughter, Amy, was eleven and excited to shop for a tallit in Jerusalem for her Bat Mitzvah. My son, Eric, was fourteen, and he wanted to ride in an army jeep and eat as many falafels as possible. Visiting Israel gave us an opportunity to pray at the Western Wall, float in the salt water of the Dead Sea, and see Yad Vashem, Israel's memorial museum to victims of the Holocaust.

We entered Yad Vashem prepared for an emotional encounter. My mother stood for a long time in front of photos, examined the faces of people walking into the camps and said, "I wonder if I'll see my parents." Those words came crashing down on me. I held my breath each time we saw photos of men and women in their fifties and sixties. And I slowly exhaled when Mom moved on to the next exhibit and added, "I don't even know if I would recognize them."

Back in 1992 the Internet was still in its infancy and finding information about those who were murdered in the Holocaust involved searching through loose-leaf pages in notebooks. The notebooks were stored in the basement of Yad Vashem, in an area far removed from visitors. The names of those who were deported and killed were all there. Finding the right notebook was not difficult. It was surprisingly simple. An elderly gentleman at the information desk pointed toward a bookshelf in the far corner. In the quiet stillness of the basement, we found:

Last Name	First Name	Date of Birth	Place of Death	Date of Death
Jacoby	Bruno	10/10/1879	Riga, Latvia	9/8/1942
Jacoby, geboren Davidsohn	Ella	06/13/1888	Riga, Latvia	9/8/1942
Jacoby	Hans Martin	11/30/1921	Auschwitz	–

There it was. Cold. Simple. Final. Even Ella's maiden name, Davidsohn, was there. We knew they had died, but seeing the names in that notebook added another level of pain. I sat with Mom on a hard bench, unable to stand, unable to move. With her eyes clouded by tears, Mom gently ran her fingers over the names.

As we walked away, I glanced at the man seated at the information desk. He looked at me with an expression of sadness and weariness. Every day, he explained, he witnessed the same thing. People came and asked about a lost relative. He could easily help them find a name, but not with the grief that followed.

Yad Vashem's database of Shoah victims has advanced greatly since the days of notebooks. Today when you search the database on the internet, you will find that Bruno and Ella were deported from Berlin on Transport 19, Train Da 403. A third-class passenger train took them away on Saturday morning, September 5, 1942. There were 804 human beings on that train, forty-seven of them under the age of 15. No one knew where they were going. The train traveled east through Poland, then north through Lithuania and Latvia. On September 8 the train came to Riga, the capital of Latvia. Riga was once a city with a thriving Jewish community, but all that changed when the Nazis occupied Latvia. A year before Bruno and Ella were deported, more than 25,000 Jews were taken out of Riga, marched into the Rumbula forest five miles away, and forced to undress and stand along the edge of mass graves, where they were machine-gunned down. When the train carrying Bruno and Ella came to a final stop, three days after leaving Berlin, eighty men were selected for hard labor. All the others were shot and buried in the Rumbula forests the day they arrived.[2]

Statistics are cold; they have no color, no soul. They overwhelm us with their enormity. We know the story of Ella and Bruno Jacoby, but many questions still remain. For decades, Mom believed her parents were deported to Theresienstadt, not Riga. The postcard sent to Klara, with her father's handwritten note, was postmarked from there.

Yet the information from Yad Vashem lists Riga as the place of death. This leaves me confused. There are missing pieces in the puzzle. Were my grandparents deported to Theresienstadt or Riga? Where did they die?

A possible explanation is that the Nazis, masters of propaganda, wanted family members to believe their relatives were taken to Theresienstadt, a "retirement-settlement," a camp for the elderly. If the information from Yad Vashem is correct and my grandparents were murdered in Riga, perhaps the postcards were deliberately mailed from Theresienstadt to disguise the truth, just as the order to bring along a suitcase for "resettlement" deceived Bruno and Ella.

Hans Martin Jacoby is also on Yad Vashem's database. The Gestapo arrested him on the streets of Berlin in February 1943. After being held in a detention center for a week, Hans was deported on February 26 in a closed cattle car, Transport 30, to Auschwitz. The following day, Hans, along with 912 women, men and children, passed under the iron archway with the words *Arbeit Macht Frei*, "Work Sets You Free." The words were false, deceitful, and malicious. If you were lucky and stayed healthy in the face of inhuman conditions, perhaps, just perhaps, you could work and stay alive. When the train stopped, 156 men and 106 women were selected for the Arbeitslager, a labor camp. The rest were murdered in the gas chambers in Auschwitz-Birkenau.[3]

Hans Martin was a healthy, strong man of twenty-one when he was deported, and he survived the first selection. He was registered, tattooed, and became prisoner number 104435. As detail-oriented as the Nazis were, they left no record of what type of work he did, but there were papers documenting that six months after he was deported, he was taken to the prison infirmary in Auschwitz-Monowitz.[4]

Auschwitz was a network of three main camps and more than forty subcamps. The first camp, Auschwitz I, included a gas chamber, crematorium, and barracks that could house up to 20,000 inmates. As the Nazis escalated deportations and executions, the original camp was expanded, and Auschwitz II, known as Auschwitz-Birkenau, became the primary killing center. With four gas chambers and four crematoriums, the smokestacks were perpetually black.

Auschwitz III was built by IG Farben, an international chemical company known for producing synthetic dyes, pharmaceuticals, and insecticides. In the 1940s the executives of Farben were searching for a facility to manufacture a synthetic rubber, Buna. They selected a site in southern Poland, near the village of Monowitz, as it had good access to roads, rail lines, water supply, and a concentration camp.

The prisoners did the heavy work of leveling the ground, digging drainage ditches, laying cables, and building roads.

Farben paid the Nazis three to four marks per day for each inmate, a fraction of what they would have paid outside workers.[5]

Auschwitz-Monowitz was originally a production site, not a compound to house prisoners. The situation changed in the summer of 1942 when an outbreak of typhus spread through the main camp. With minimal toilet and washing facilities, the sanitation conditions were atrocious. Concerned over losing their labor force, the managers of IG Farben transferred thousands of prisoners to barracks in Auschwitz III.

The working conditions at Monowitz were as severe as any other camp. Most prisoners survived only three months. When starvation and disease stole their physical strength, the men were murdered in the gas chambers.

IG Farben deserves a special place in hell, a space next to Hitler, Himmler, and Goebbels. Not only did IG Farben operate a factory with prisoners of a concentration camp, this international chemical company manufactured Zyklon B, hydrogen cyanide, the poison that killed over a million people in Auschwitz-Birkenau.

Six months after Hans Martin was imprisoned, six months after he became Number 104435, he was sent to the Auschwitz-Monowitz infirmary. This I learned from the International Tracing Service, now known as the Arolsen Archives. Millions of documents are housed in Bad Arolsen, a small rural town in central Germany. There, original documents offer a direct link to parents, grandparents, aunts, and uncles, to relatives we want to remember.

From the archives, I have a copy of Hans Martin's identification card, the list of names from Transport 30, and his prisoner registration form. The form states that he was 164 centimeters, 5 feet 4 inches, he had an appendectomy scar on the right side of his stomach, his teeth were in good condition with one crown made of precious metal, and he spoke three languages, German, French, and English.

There is also a list of dates of admission to the Krankenbau, the infirmary, and dates of discharge or death. The first time Hans Martin was sent to the infirmary was on September 14, 1943.

Being in the infirmary carried an uncertain fate. For those with a severe injury, the end was imminent. But if there was an infection that could be resolved with sulfa drugs or a wound that could heal quickly, a few days in the infirmary could make a man productive again and keep him alive. While there is no information on what brought him to the infirmary, Hans was discharged after a week of rest and medical attention. However, he returned on October 26 and again on December 27, perhaps for a new medical ailment or the same illness that was never resolved. Each time, he was released after a week.[6]

Neither the Arolsen Archives or the Auschwitz Museum has any documents of what happened to Hans after he was discharged for the third time on January 1, 1944. The Yad Vashem database lists Hans as "declared dead," but without a place or date of death.

All the pieces of this puzzle may never come together as boxes of files were lost or burned as the war came to an end. For me, the piece that burns in my soul and makes my heart ache is that Hans Martin survived until liberation, but never made it home.

In the long-forgotten days before Hitler, Hans Martin loved sports, told funny stories, and made everyone laugh. People liked him and even in the brutal world of the camps, Hans found a Nazi with a sympathetic soul. Twice this man mailed out notes to Klara, handwritten by Hans, asking for food. And three times, the SS guards brought Hans to the infirmary, not the gas chambers. Someone with authority wanted him to recover. Someone wanted him to live.

Hans Martin's life in the camps was touched by a few compassionate people. But like so many others, he didn't survive. The vast evil of the Nazi machine overwhelmed the traces of good.

* * *

Life after the war slowly resumed a routine, a new normal. Ernst found a way to support his mother, Lilo, and himself in the market. He traded with Russian soldiers, knowing they were eager to purchase watches and cameras, as well as cigarettes and chocolates. He thought about enrolling in the university to complete his education, but it was not the right time. There were too many obligations, too many responsibilities, and a need for financial security. During the years in hiding, cash meant survival. It meant paying outrageous prices for food on the black market. There would be another time to return to school.

Lilo started a vocational program at the Lette Schule, a school for young women offering training in dressmaking, cooking, and bookkeeping. Lilo loved clothes and fashion, and through the classes, she learned how to use a sewing machine, transform sketches into patterns, and turn a bolt of cloth into a tailored dress.

The time after the war was a period of waiting to leave for America. Betty made the journey at the end of January 1947 with assistance from the Hebrew Immigrant Aid Society. HIAS arranged the visa and purchased a ticket for Betty to board the SS *Marine Perch* and reunite with her older son Gerhard who was living in New Jersey.

While Betty, Ernst and Lilo lived together for more than a year and a half after the war, the two women never formed a warm connection. There weren't angry words, rather periods of silence and coldness that never disappeared.

It was only after Betty had moved to America that Ernst and Lilo began speaking of marriage. Without the underlying tension, Lilo could imagine a future with Ernst. He had always wanted her to be his wife, and in time, Lilo agreed.

On March 29, 1947, Ernst Egon Joseph married Elisabeth Charlotte Lena Jacoby. Their wedding photograph shows the newlyweds walking arm-in-arm out of the registrar's office after the civil ceremony. Lilo is radiant, a beautiful smiling bride, wearing a stylish fur coat, a wide-brimmed hat, and open-toed sandals. Ernst is also smiling, not a wide grin, which is not his nature, but a clear, firm smile and a steady, optimistic gaze towards the future. He looks handsome in a dark overcoat, white shirt, and striped tie. There are two ladies in the background, two witnesses to the ceremony. The one on the left, the shorter lady, is Erika Krause. Erika was Ernst's cousin and his only relative in Berlin. She survived the war protected by her German husband, but her parents were deported and murdered at Auschwitz.[7] The taller lady is Gerdi Asbach. Lilo had no relatives to stand by her side that day, only Gerdi, the artist who lived in Mrs. Sotscheck's house. I'm certain that Gerdi passed a quick wink and a warm smile to Frau Joseph as she walked out the door.

In the months following the wedding, Ernst and Lilo spent hours talking about coming to the United States, to Trenton, N.J. where Gerhard lived with his American wife and their two little girls.

* * *

Gerhard came to America in June 1938, after graduating from the University of Berlin with a doctorate in law and economics. He traveled on a visitor's visa, which only allowed a two-week stay. To remain permanently he needed to have a sponsor, someone willing to sign an Affidavit of Support.

In his narrative of the journey, Gerhard wrote, "I arrived in New York on schedule on Thursday, June 2. The Immigration Inspector took one look at my passport and said only two words, 'Ellis Island.'"

Gerhard knew this might happen. Friends in Germany warned him he would never get into America, that officials would detain him and send him back to Germany.

After a night at Ellis Island, Gerhard sat across the table from the immigration board. They were skeptical. They didn't believe he would return to Germany in two weeks, but they came up with an agreement, as Gerhard explained: "They would let me go ashore if I would post a bond of $500 cash on the barrel head to ensure I would leave the country as I said I would. They would not accept checks or German marks or notes or anything else. It had to be 500 American dollars. Where was I going to get that kind of money? In desperation I called the North German Lloyd office."

That was the shipping company that brought him to America. Gerhard had paid for a trip that included hotel, meals, and admission to the Empire State Building and Rockefeller Center, and there he was, confined in Ellis Island.

Of course, Gerhard had not come to America to be a tourist. I suspect that he purchased a visitor's package to reinforce his intention of a limited stay in America, not because he planned on a sightseeing excursion.

In a fortunate turn of events, North German Lloyd agreed to post the bond, and they also extended the date for the return trip from June 15 to June 22. Early Monday morning, after four days at Ellis Island, Gerhard was free to leave.

There is nothing in my uncle's notes of his first impression of Manhattan, walking the streets, gazing upward at the skyscrapers, or seeing the diversity of people crowding the buses and subways. Instead, he pulled out the list of names given him by friends and professors in Germany and started making phone calls.

When my uncle came in 1938, the U.S. was still working itself out of the Great Depression, and the unemployment rate was 19 percent.[8] Antisemitism was also a factor. Universities used quotas to restrict Jewish admission, and banks redlined neighborhoods to prevent Jews from moving in.

In the political arena, elected officials opposed an increase in immigration quotas. Isolationist senators and congressmen believed that "our first duty is to our own people" and that immigrants would "take jobs that Americans are now holding."[9]

Gerhard came to the U.S. clearly understanding the high unemployment numbers and antisemitism, but even more so, he knew the desperate situation back home. Millions of men and women were unemployed in the U.S., but the situation there held no comparison to the conditions in Germany. Americans were focused on their own domestic issues and pushed aside the problems in Europe.

By June 15, Gerhard had not found a sponsor. With a week remaining before he had to return to Germany, a contact in New Rochelle suggested he contact Victor Cooper, who lived in Trenton, New Jersey,

Mr. Cooper was a self-educated man who owned a network of oil and gas distribution companies and gas stations. He had made a fortune during Prohibition operating breweries and beer warehouses. Finding a place for a drink in Trenton in the 1920s was not difficult, especially since William Walter, Trenton's chief of police and Mr. Cooper's close friend, often turned a blind eye on beer-run distributors and speakeasies throughout the city.[10]

Gerhard arrived at the gas station where the meeting had been arranged and explained his situation. Mr. Cooper asked no questions. He simply agreed to sign the Affidavit.

In his notes, my uncle provided some background to make sense of why Mr. Cooper was willing to help a stranger. A week before Gerhard came to America, the newspapers ran a story about a man from Germany who was detained at Ellis Island. Rather than return home, this man committed suicide by jumping out a window. Mr. Cooper vowed to help the next person in the same situation.[11]

Gerhard now had a handshake and a promise, but no document. It would take a few weeks to get the papers finalized, but without the affidavit, Gerhard needed to be out of the U.S. by June 22. The U.S. immigration office didn't stipulate where he went, just that he leave the county. In his notes, Gerhard wrote, "[Mr. Cooper] warned me about going back to Germany, saying that the Nazis were sure to arrest me and send me to a concentration camp. He suggested that I go to either Canada or Cuba and wait."

Gerhard heeded Mr. Cooper's advice and made his way by bus to Miami and boarded a boat to Cuba. On June 21, he landed in Havana in time to satisfy the agreement made at Ellis Island, and protect $500 for North German Lloyd.

Victor Cooper was good for his word, but it took more than a month for the papers to arrive. In early August, Gerhard returned to Miami, then back on a bus to Trenton, where Mr. Cooper offered him a job. Gerhard pumped gas at the service station for a day, then worked in the office and remained with Mr. Cooper for eight and a half years.

During his four days detained in Ellis Island, my uncle found a lucky charm, a four-leaf clover. Just as divine intervention or luck protected my father as he walked the streets of Berlin, perhaps this four-leaf clover came to my uncle at the exact right moment.

A year after Betty left for America, the immigration and visa papers came for Ernst and Lilo. Many in Berlin had already gone to America, often to Brooklyn or the Bronx, but no one to Trenton. Ernst unfolded a large map of the United States to see where their new home would be. At least it wasn't too far from Philadelphia or New York, and since it was the capital of New Jersey, Lilo hoped there would be a theater and some nice stores.

Weeks before their trip, Ernst brought English newspapers home. He and Lilo had studied English in school, and they had a good command of vocabulary. Even so, they practiced reading and reviewed grammar books. But there's so much more to language than lessons in a textbook. Soon after coming to America, Lilo learned that a smile and "Hello" were a much better greeting than "Pleased to make your acquaintance."

As the trip approached, Ernst packed the steamer trunk with clothes they would need and items they valued. He placed the heavy silverware in sturdy boxes. The set included a service for twelve plus ice cream spoons, fish knives, and tiny espresso coffee spoons, pieces they might never need, but Ernst had purchased it as a good investment in silver. Extra care was taken with the Bing and Grondahl gray porcelain vase from Mrs. Sotscheck and Gerdi's painting. Gerdi's wedding present was a watercolor of four lilies, three pale peach flowers, and one bright white lily standing tall against a soft blue background. On the back, she wrote:

Zum Hochzeitstag! Zur Erinnerung an gemeinsame schwere und schöne Stunden. Gerdi! am 19. III.47

For the wedding day! In memory of the difficult and good times we shared together. Gerdi! March 19, 1947

Lilo packed her warm beaver coat, woolen sweaters, and plaid skirts. She had some jewelry from her mother, a gold brooch with a delicate chain, an oval amethyst ring set in a wide gold band, and a coral necklace. There wasn't much to bring, just the few things she and Hans had carried in their pockets after her parents were deported. Twice they had tiptoed back into the apartment after the Gestapo had sealed the door, after their parents were taken to Grosse Hamburger Strasse. Each piece was wrapped in tissue paper and tucked deep inside her handbag along with a handful of family photos.

Before closing the apartment door for the last time, Ernst checked and re-checked all the necessary documents and placed them in a secure briefcase along with his Leica camera. They traveled by train to Bremen and waited in a displaced persons camp for about three weeks until it was time to board the SS *Marine Flasher*. Just as HIAS had helped Betty, the American Joint Distribution Committee (later known as JDC) supported Ernst and Lilo, and on June 15, 1948, the ship set sail for New York City.

With choppy waters and unseasonably cold weather, Lilo and Ernst spent many days on deck wrapped in warm coats, plus a few down below battling seasickness. In the early morning of June 25, as the sun was just rising, they caught their first glimpse of the Statue of Liberty. As the lady in the harbor with her torch held high came into view, the boat erupted in cheers. Men waved their hats, women pulled out handkerchiefs to wipe away tears, and small groups broke out singing "America the Beautiful."

Ernst stared into the ocean remembering the night he placed his father into the river. Lilo gazed at the passengers, strangers who looked familiar, and rested her eyes on an elderly couple, holding on to each other for support, and a young man nearby, laughing and smiling at everyone.

Ernst and Lilo walked off the boat carrying their suitcases and the souls of those who didn't survive and stepped onto the shores of America.

Elisabeth Joseph

Ernst Joseph

Bertha ("Betty") Joseph

Wedding Photo - Elisabeth and Ernst Joseph, March
29, 1947; Standing in the back, left to right, Erika
Krause and Gerdi Asbach

8

LIFE IN AMERICA

Ernst and Lilo stepped off the SS *Marine Flasher* and searched the crowd for a familiar face. Ernst had not seen his brother for ten years, and Lilo had never met him. At the end of the long exit ramp Lilo spotted her mother-in-law, and standing by her side was a man she immediately recognized: Gerhard had the same fair complexion, piercing blue eyes, and thinning blond hair as his brother. He held up both arms in welcome, then moved aside to give space to a lady standing next to him holding a bouquet of roses. Lux Emmerich, Lilo's closest friend in Germany, had come to America a year ago and was now married and living in Manhattan. The time in Auschwitz remained hidden inside this beautiful young woman standing on the dock to welcome her friend.

As soon as Ernst and Lilo had cleared customs, Gerhard brought everyone back to his home in Trenton. The city boasted a gold-domed capital building by the Delaware River, a downtown shopping district with restaurants, a movie theater, department stores, and a train station where the Pennsylvania Railroad brought commuters to Manhattan in just over an hour.

Since arriving in America a year earlier, Betty had been living with her older son on 723 Edgewood Avenue. The two-story, red-brick, semi-detached house was a few blocks from Cadwalader Park. On Sunday mornings, the balloon man stood at the park entrance and welcomed families into the park, and kids dashed off to see the monkeys and feed the ducks and geese swimming in the pond. It was a perfect place to play for Gerhard's children, Judi, age six, and Barbara, age three.

Miriam, Gerhard's wife, helped Ernst and Lilo settle into their room, previously an attic but now a fully furnished bedroom. Barbara scampered up the steps, fascinated with Lilo's bright red nails, and called out, "Polish, polish . . . nail polish!" Lilo opened her cosmetic bag filled with an assortment of colored nail polishes, and Judi and Barbara spent the afternoon giggling and admiring their brightly painted fingers and toes.

There were now two more German speakers in the house, a tremendous relief to Betty. Miriam, who had grown up in Trenton, spoke Yiddish, which helped, but Betty was far more comfortable speaking and thinking in German.

JDC, the relief organizations that supplied funds for Ernst and Lilo and thousands of others to board passenger ships and come to America, partnered with other Jewish agencies to provide social welfare services to the new arrivals. Understanding the needs of immigrants extended far beyond transportation, JDC worked with the United Service for New Americans, USNA, to help the newcomers adjust to life in America.

Ann S. Petluck, Director for Migration Services for USNA, reported that Lilo and Ernst immediately found employment.

Lilo began working on July 5 and Ernst on July 10. They worked in factories, Ernst as a cutter of rubber heels and soles, and Lilo as a seamstress. By the end of the year, Ernst was earning $44 a week at Essex Rubber Corp. and Lilo was earning $29 a week at Philmac Sportswear.[1]

In her memo to the agency, Ms. Petluck wrote, "Mr. and Mrs. Joseph have been entirely self-supporting since July 15, 1948. [. . .] They have made a good vocational adjustment and have participated in community activities for the newcomer. Both have received their first papers for American citizenship. We have been informed that they have not received any public relief and have not been inmates of a public institution."[2]

Ms. Petluck's report reassured the U.S. immigration office that there was no reason to worry; these folks were law-abiding and did not require welfare. Three weeks were all they needed to become self-sufficient.

As welcoming as Gerhard and Miriam were, the house on Edgewood Avenue was small for seven people. Ernst wanted his own place, and early in autumn, he and Lilo moved into a third-floor walk-up on West Ingham Avenue, a street with vacant lots, broken sidewalks and without front lawns. The shortcomings were easily overcome by the rent of $23 per month for a fully furnished apartment and an optimism that this home would be the beginning of a better life in America.

There was one major drawback: no private bathroom. The bathroom was out in the hallway and shared with other tenants. Even this inconvenience was initially accepted but turned into a greater issue when Lilo became pregnant. In the spring of 1950, Ernst and Lilo moved out of Ingham Avenue and into a first-floor apartment on Market Street. Dr. Bloom, the dentist who owned the building, lived on the second floor and rented out the apartment behind his office. The neighborhood was largely Jewish, and many were Holocaust survivors with numbers on their left arm.

Living on Market Street was definitely a step up. Lilo was now pregnant, and it was nice to have an apartment with their own bathroom, plus a porch outside the front door for a baby carriage.

Lilo hoped the baby would be a girl. She believed that boys were too vulnerable. It was too easy to lose a son in war; a girl would be safer. Even without military service, Lilo believed that a boy would grow up, fall in love, get married, and move away. A daughter, Lilo thought, would always stay with her. Ernst was not at all concerned over the sex of the baby. He was worried about money. Would he be able to provide for his child? Even before the baby was born, Ernst was calculating the cost of college.

On July 26, 1950, Lilo's wish came true. She gave birth to a healthy baby girl. She named me Evelyn Linda Joseph, to carry on the memory of her mother, Ella, and Ernst's father, Leopold.

* * *

In 1953, as soon as my parents satisfied the five-year residency requirement, they took the U.S. Naturalization Test and became American citizens. Under oath, they proudly declared to "support and defend the Constitution and laws of the United States of America against all enemies, foreign and domestic."

My father tried to fully embrace American culture. He wanted English, only English, to be spoken in the house. He knew of families whose children had to repeat kindergarten because they didn't know the language. That would not happen to his daughter.

But he couldn't totally separate himself from the past, and German words found their way into the house. My father read every article in the *Aufbau*, the weekly German newspaper, and he spoke to my grandmother, my Oma, in German, and sometimes to my mother when he didn't want me to understand. I can hear my father singing "*Muss I denn, muss I denn zum Städtele hinaus*," a popular German song about a soldier going off to war and promising to be faithful to the girl he leaves behind. The melody is upbeat and made its way to an American audience through Elvis Presley. Elvis adapted the melody and released the song "Wooden Heart" in 1964, with verses in German and English.

My parents had studied English in school, but Oma didn't have that advantage. She spoke only German, yet I understood her. Language is funny that way. Understanding is easier than speaking. I grew up with a grasp of "kitchen German," the language women used at home. I picked up phrases and could follow conversations, but the rules of grammar remained a mystery.

To so many people, the German language is the harsh sounds of Hitler's speeches. Watching videos of Hitler addressing massive crowds with young men holding their arms up high, shouting, "*Sieg Heil . . .Heil Hitler*," gives me a visceral chill. It is painful to listen to the driving force of Hitler's words, to the cadence that turned rational men into Nazis. To many Americans, this is the sound of German. It is bitter, it is coarse, and it is cruel.

Yet, I also hear other sounds, songs and phrases such as, *"Es wird schon wieder besser,"* Things will be better. Mom says those words when she doesn't feel well or when something is not going right. It is an all-purpose phrase of optimism.

I have wonderful memories from when I was growing up in Trenton, especially of shopping trips with Mom. We'd start walking up the hill from our house on Market Street, turn left onto Broad Street, and continue down to the corner of State and Broad, the center of the city. It was about a mile, but to a little girl, it seemed like a long journey. We'd look at the clothes in the windows of Arnold Constable and Nevius-Voorhees on East State Street, and S. P. Dunham's on North Broad Street. Those were the clothes to admire, not to buy. Mom and I entered the stores on a mission. We were there to search the sales racks for a bargain. Most often we'd leave with a bag in our hands, and then stop for soda at the counter in Woolworth's before going home.

The city had reached its economic peak a decade or two before my parents' arrival. That was when the Roebling steel mills dominated the area, but the city I knew in the 1950s was still thriving. Factories, especially in the rubber industry, were hiring more workers and the General Motors manufacturing plant in Ewing Township was expanding, bringing workers and families to the suburbs.

Trenton's Jewish community at that time was large enough to support a half dozen synagogues, from Orthodox to Reform, a Young Men's Hebrew Association (YMHA, a precursor to today's Jewish Community Center), a Jewish day school, and an old age home.

We didn't own a car, but it was easy to get around by foot or bus. My father frequently took me on trips to the bank, and we often came home with a toaster, a blanket, or an alarm clock, gifts offered as incentives to open accounts.

In those days, banks were grand, formal-looking buildings with spacious interiors, high ceilings, and dark mahogany furniture. My father would lift me up onto the marble countertop while he filled out the deposit slip (never a withdrawal). I was four years old, and I remember feeling quite elegant and royal sitting on a throne next to my father.

As a young child, I learned the power of money had nothing to do with what it could buy, but rather with how much was saved. If I asked for something, my father would say, "Do you need it, or do you want it?" I quickly learned the difference, and even to this day, his words have stayed with me.

Those early memories of trips to the department store with my mother and to the bank with my father speak clearly about who my parents were. However, I don't want to give the impression that my mother was extravagant, quite the contrary. My mother shopped for clothes on sale and proudly told my father how much she saved on each item. Sadly, that never impressed him. He never appreciated her efforts, never noticed a new blouse or offered a compliment on a pretty dress.

The love and affection my father once had for my mother had disappeared. Working in a factory was not what he originally imagined, and I believe that left him bitter and unhappy, and those emotions spilled over into their marriage.

My mother never shared that early love for my father. She entered into marriage as the best alternative given the loss of her family. She often said she would never have married my father if her brother had survived. Each time I heard those words, I felt a twinge of pain and a stab of sadness. But my heart also ached whenever I saw my mother in tears, and as much as I tried to console her, I knew that both my mother and father had found words to deeply hurt each other.

* * *

In those early years, our closest friends were a German-Jewish family living on Union Street just around the corner from us. Erich and Hetti Jacobs and their son, Jethro, fled Germany in September 1941. They spent more than four years in Havana, Cuba, before being allowed to enter America.[3] Their daughter Fredel was born in the U.S., and through the friendship of our mothers, Fredel and I became good friends. The family was Orthodox, strictly following the dietary laws and observing Shabbat as a day of rest and prayer. My earliest introduction to Judaism came through the Jacobs family. I have been at many Passover Seders, but none lasted longer or left a deeper impression than the night Mr. Jacobs brought out his old, worn notebook and expanded the traditional Haggadah with countless commentaries and stories.

Our shared German-Jewish background formed the bond of our friendship. Many of our other Jewish neighbors came from eastern Europe and spoke Yiddish, a factor that separated us from them.

When Mom came to the U.S. and heard Yiddish for the first time, her reaction was, "They speak such a poor German."

The disconnect to Yiddish is part of my parents' German-Jewish identity and a challenge to understand. As a child, I considered my parents peculiar for not rejecting their German past. In time I learned that my parents were not strange, but rather typical of

German Jews, proud of their cultural background, and I've come to share that pride.

Over the years, Mom has known many Holocaust survivors, often from Poland or Hungary. Some have looked directly at her and said, "Not you personally, but German Jews always felt they were better than us."

Thinking about their words, Mom said to me, "We lived in Berlin, not a little shtetl, everything was there. We could get an education, even go to college . . . So maybe it was true, maybe we always felt we were better."

Perhaps the most significant factor in our friendship with the Jacobs family was that they understood that not all Germans were Nazis, a concept so important to my father as expressed in his notes:

I wanted to write mainly for one reason to show that not all the German people were bad or indifferent to what happened to the Jewish people. I have to praise them highly and say that my life was saved by some members of the same German nation, who destroyed millions of European Jews. My family and I were saved from the Nazis by German gentile people, who risked their lives and their family's lives to help us. The reason for this writing is to honor them and not to forget their noble deeds.[4]

Neighbors on Market Street started to move away when they could afford homes in the suburbs. We joined the exodus when my father purchased an apartment house on 135 Francis Avenue, in Hamilton Township. We still didn't have a car, or a TV, but we owned an investment property.

The houses on Francis Avenue were one-family homes and small apartment buildings, all on neatly cut front lawns. In 1955, a handful of our neighbors were Jewish, but most were Italian-Catholic.

All the apartment houses looked the same: red-brick and stucco two-story buildings with four units. Two large fir trees on our front lawn provided a shady place for me to play on hot summer days. The front door opened into a small vestibule with a door to the basement and a panel of mailboxes on the side wall. We lived on the first floor, and I had a bedroom with flowered wallpaper and a window that looked out to a swing set in the fenced-in backyard.

There were two twin beds in my room, one on either side with a narrow space between them. I slept on the bed against the wall common to the tenants in the other apartment. They were an elderly couple who frequently went out in the evening, came home drunk, and argued for hours. I couldn't make out their words, but their voices were loud and kept me awake. Rolling away from the wall, I faced the other bed, where Oma was snoring and sleeping soundly. After a few good "Uh hmms," the room became quiet and I drifted off to sleep.

My grandmother came to stay with us after Uncle Gerhard and his family moved away. My uncle's house was far larger than ours, and Oma would have stayed with him if not for his new job in Ohio. Gerhard had progressed through a number of positions since arriving in America. After many years with Victor Cooper, he found employment with the American Joint Distribution Committee in New York. Working with the JDC, Gerhard had been able to facilitate the paperwork required to bring my parents to the U.S.

Next came a job with a local radio station, WTTM, and after a few years there, he received an offer from Air Trails Network, a company centered in the Midwest. The new job, a better position, brought him to the manager's desk at WING and the family resettled in Dayton.[5]

Without cousins, an aunt, or uncle our family was very small. I asked for a baby brother or sister many times, and although that never happened, Mom took on the role of parent and friend. She taught me to swim, ride a bike, and jump the waves in the ocean at Asbury Park. On many summer afternoons, we pedaled off to Woodlawn Pool to escape the heat. I remember watching Mom climb up the steps to the high-diving board, stand tall on the edge, toes and arms extended, glance down at me, and perform a perfect dive.

Mom had a knack for making the ordinary feel special, and with the help of *My Fair Lady* spinning on the record player, dusting turned into dance. Through the music and lyrics of Lerner and Loewe, we chasséd around the living room with dust cloths extended and practiced our plies. We sang along with Eliza Doolittle wishing for "a room far away from the cold night air," which made me think about the war years and Mom's nights without a bed.

Next came "With a Little Bit of Luck," another song that had meaning far beyond the boundaries of the show. Then came the showstopper, the song we played over and over until the scratches on the vinyl became part of the melody. When "I Could Have Danced all Night" started playing, we gave up any pretense of cleaning and simply twirled around the room. Mom's memories went back to a pre-Hitler time of ballet, and my adolescent thoughts raced towards a future of imagined romance. My dad, a serious man and an excellent provider, had no interest in dance, and I became Mom's ballroom partner.

Dance was one of many differences between my parents. Mom was an extrovert who enjoyed dressing up and going out, and she judged others on their appearance and social charms. Mom's easy bantering with men irritated Dad. There was tension in the house, many angry words exchanged and long periods of silence. While I loved my dad, the fights between them brought me to mom's defense, and I became her protector. I took on this role as a child and continued as an adult.

When I was eight years old, Dad changed jobs and began working at the U.S. Post Office. Pay, benefits, and conditions were all an improvement over factory work. Dad sorted mail during the afternoon shift, which gave him time in the mornings to take care of the apartments. There were now eight units, as he owned a second building on Francis Avenue. Maintenance and repairs were a never-ending chore. I can see Dad in the basement, standing by his workbench and searching for the right size washer to fix a leaky faucet, climbing the ladder to paint the shutters, checking out the roof for broken shingles, and on many hot, humid days, pushing the manual lawn mower.

Dad considered buying an investment property in the Bronx or Brooklyn. He looked at many five- or six-story buildings, with 20 or more units; some were walk-ups, others had elevators. Investing in one of these properties would be a quantum leap from real estate in Hamilton Township. Dad devoted weekends to inspecting properties and hours reviewing cashflow statements, each one advertising strong profits. My father would have loved to own real estate in New York, if the right one came along, but it never did.

* * *

Oma always wore a dress, corset, stockings, and sensible shoes. I don't believe she owned a pair of pants. We understood each other, often in ways that required few words, such as sitting on the couch and turning the pages of *Life*, a weekly news magazine with more photos than articles. Oma lived with us for a few months, less than a year, before taking a job as a live-in companion for an elderly German lady in Manhattan. I don't know if she had ever worked before, but I remember her being quite happy when we visited her on Sunday afternoons. As Oma grew older and no longer felt able to care for someone else, she moved back to Trenton. She rented a second-floor apartment with a sunny kitchen and spacious living room a block away from Cadwalader Park. Each time I walked up the flight of stairs on the side of the house, I could smell the fragrance of tea and cookies mingled with 4711 Eau de Cologne.

One warm Thursday afternoon in June 1962, a day that felt more like summer than spring, Oma never returned our phone calls. Dad had taken her to the family doctor that morning for a routine appointment. Oma had diabetes, but managed to control it with daily insulin injections and regular medical visits. The doctor was pleased with her blood sugar numbers and found nothing else of concern.

That afternoon Oma died from a heart attack. She was seventy-one, an age considered elderly at that time, yet I never thought of her as old. Her passing was my first encounter with death, and I grieved the loss of a grandmother. For Dad the loss was sharp and mingled with anger at his perception that the medical community failed his mother.

Oma never fully adjusted to life in America. My father served as a bridge, connecting her in language and sharing memories of living in hiding. Dad's day-to-day life was filled with obligations, but in quiet moments, he suffered the loss of his mother and blamed the doctor for his grief.

At the time Oma died, my parents were looking at houses on the market. This time the search was for a single-family house. They had weekly appointments with a realtor to meet the deadline of my Bat Mitzvah in June 1963. This religious milestone also meant that Uncle Gerhard and family would be coming in from Dayton, and my parents wanted to be in a nice home, a sign of the financial security they had achieved.

After checking out dozens of properties, my parents put a deposit on 411 Vannest Avenue in Ewing Township, a colonial house with woods in the backyard, a breezeway that connected the garage to the kitchen, the best place to hang out after school, and much more space than we ever had in the apartment.

Days after trucks delivered the furniture, my parents sat in the first row at Brothers of Israel, a conservative synagogue on Greenwood Avenue, and listened as I chanted the Haftorah and led the congregation in prayers and songs on Friday night.

Through Hebrew school classes on Tuesday and Thursday afternoons, plus Sunday mornings, I had learned to read Hebrew and chant the prayers. Brothers of Israel provided a religious home, a community, a place to belong.

Trips between Dayton and Trenton were reserved for special occasions, and my Bat Mitzvah qualified as a reason for the family to be together. We celebrated with a family lunch in our new house, but for me, a girl of thirteen, the highlight was a teenage party in the backyard on Saturday night, complete with paper lanterns, records, and deli sandwiches.

* * *

The house on Vannest Avenue was less than a mile from Ewing High School. Most days I walked, but sometimes I drove Dad's car, a 1958 sky-blue and white Plymouth sedan with pushbutton transmission and classic tailfins, large as a boat, impossible to parallel park, and so much fun to drive.

Dad and I had been math buddies for years. Beginning in grammar school, he insisted I learn the new lessons before they were introduced in class. On Sunday afternoons, we sat down at the kitchen table with pencil, paper, and lots of erasers, and began working out problems in the upcoming chapter. It was our special bond, plus there was a bonus of doing well on tests. High school algebra and geometry were rather straightforward, but calculus presented some tricky problems. Those homework questions I left for Dad. He was still working the afternoon shift at the U.S. Post Office and coming home after 11 pm. Mom had a midnight snack ready, but before eating, he'd sit down and work out the steps to solve the hard problems, the ones no other kid in class got right.

In my senior year, I received an academic scholarship from the Post Office. The scholarship brought Dad congratulations from co-workers, and validated his belief in me. Every year Ewing High recognized one senior in each academic subject, and in 1968, I received this honor from the English department. Mom took great pleasure that her daughter, a child of German immigrants, received this award.

In September, I loaded my packed suitcases into the family car, and my parents drove me off to college in New Brunswick. Douglass College, the women's division of Rutgers University, was only an hour away, but for me, it was far beyond the horizon of home.

Freshman year was consumed with exploration and the freedom of time organized by my own interests. As a pre-med major, I was enrolled in required courses in chemistry and biology, but academics took a back seat to a social life. Freshmen year grades were mediocre as too many hours were devoted to late-night dorm conversations and time listening to tracks on *Bookends*, singing along with Simon & Garfunkel's wistful lyrics about exploring America while counting the cars on the New Jersey Turnpike.

My priorities began to shift in sophomore year and by junior year, I was much better at managing time between lectures, labs, and a part-time job in the college infirmary, where I learned to read sed rates and hematocrits. That was the year I met Lenny at the Douglass College library. Leonard Grossman, a pre-med major, was tall and lanky, with deep brown eyes and chin-length curly brown hair. We shared a bacteriology class on the Rutgers campus, and as we drove back from class in his 1962 blue convertible Volkswagen, I learned that he loved classical music and played trumpet with the Rutgers Wind Ensemble and the Rutgers Marching Band.

There was classical music playing in the house the day Lenny came to meet my parents. Actually, classical music was always in the house, either from one of my father's many records or from the Blaupunkt table radio. As my father walked down the stairs to say hello, Lenny greeted him and without hesitation, he identified the piece as the first movement of Beethoven's Eighth Symphony. My father smiled and extended his hand in welcome.

* * *

My parents' past had receded into a corner of our lives that didn't require much attention until a letter from Oscar Materne, written in December 1962, demanded the past be remembered. Materne wrote:

Liebe Frau Joseph, Lieber Ernst,

Durch unsere langen Bekanntschaft . . . wäre es doch von Ihnen angebracht gewesen und etwas von sich hören zu lassen, denn man war ja schließlich kein 'Niemand.' [6]

Dear Mrs. Joseph, Dear Ernst,

Because of our long friendship . . . it would have been appropriate to hear from you, because after all, I was not a "Nobody."

"*Niemand*" jumps off the page, larger than any other word in the handwritten letter. I believe Materne was screaming with frustration and disappointment that my father had failed to treat him with the respect he deserved and angry over years of silence. The letter continued with reference to their shared history:

Es lag ja schließlich eine Geschichte unter uns Dreien in den so vielen Fahren unserer Bekanntschaft. Ich weiß nicht, ob Sie noch Wert darauf legen?

After all, there was a story among the three of us, so many ways of our connection. I don't know if you care?

Materne ended the letter with a desire to rekindle their friendship:

Möchte noch so vielen mitteilen aber ich weiß nicht, ob Sie diese Zeilen erreichen.

There's so much I want to share with you, but I'm not sure if you will receive this letter.

The envelope was addressed to my father and Frau B. Joseph (Oma, not Mom) at 723 Edgewood Avenue. I am not sure how long it took the letter to reach my father, but what is most surprising is that it ever was received, considering my parents had not lived on Edgewood Avenue for more than ten years.

Perhaps a co-worker at the post office connected my father to the name on the envelope, but that is just speculation.

In November 1964, Dad replied:

Dear Oscar,

It is really true, after a long silence, a sign of life. I don't know how long we haven't heard from each other. We have drifted apart, and yet we still have so much in common. I'm writing you this letter, but I don't know if you will receive it. I hope so . . . A long time has passed since we saw each other. More than 16 years. The time here for us has passed very quickly, too quickly. Hard to believe. How happy I would be to hear from you, to know how you and your wife are doing.

How often I have wanted to write, but it has always escaped me. Now my guilty conscience gives me no rest. Dear Oscar, let me hear from you, and forgive me my long silence . . . I know you are no longer a youngster, and it is likely that you are no longer working. If there is something you want that I can do, please let me know. Who knows how long we can still help.

When was it last that we heard from each other? I don't know anymore, and I can't ask my dear mother. She is no longer with us. More than two years ago, in June 1962, she passed away.

You have no idea how often we think about you, and how often we talk about you. Forget the long time we haven't talked, and let us be old friends again, as we were before. You have no idea how happy that would make me.

Stay well, you and your wife.

Best wishes from me, who has never forgotten you.

Ernst

If you are in East Berlin, let me know so I can send you something.

Once more, best wishes.[7]

Materne lived on Schwartskopffstrasse 8, a small street in East Berlin, a few blocks from the Berlin Wall.

When the war came to an end, the Allies agreed to divide Germany into four occupied zones. The Russian zone became East Germany, and the three sections separately controlled by the United States, Great Britain, and France consolidated into West Germany. Berlin, the capital city, was similarly divided even though the city itself was entirely within East Germany.

Over time, thousands of people fled from East to West Germany via Berlin. Dissatisfied with life under a communist system, many Germans, especially the young and well-educated left for better paying jobs and modern apartments and to escape the watchful eye of the Stasi, the secret police.

To prevent continued migration, the East German government built the wall and as a consequence, families were separated and life became especially onerous for those in the east.

Two months after Ernst mailed his letter, a reply came:

Dear Mr. Joseph,

Ernst, today I'm finding the time to answer your letter. Unfortunately, I must write that my dear, good Oscar died on February 8, 1964, after a long illness. At that time, I lost him forever. My biggest satisfaction is my trip to the cemetery, to his gravesite. He was sick and in a hospital for a year. Even though I knew he was ill, and I was prepared, his passing came too quickly. My Oscar would have been happy to receive a Lebenszeichen (life sign) from you; but your letter came too late.

Since I only get a small pension, I would be very thankful if you sent a small food package.

I don't have to pay tax, since I get a pension. But you must write on the package, "Pensioner."

I hope the New Year started off well, that you are healthy and everything is going well.

Best wishes,

Yours,

Martha Materne[8]

That was the beginning of years of correspondence. Dad saved Frau Materne's letters, handwritten on yellow lined paper, and kept copies of his own typed replies on onionskin. Each note was tucked inside a box of food packed with items the East German government allowed. Cans were not permitted, and with regret, my father wrote he could not include canned meat.

Knowing it was highly likely that the Stasi opened the boxes, Dad included a list of contents as reference. With minimal variation, the boxes contained:

1 Glass Nescafe- 6 ounces

2 Cartons of tea bags- 96; 7 ½ ounces

1 Package Cocoa

1 Package of Dates without Pits- 1 pound

1 Package of fig cookies- 2 pounds

1 Package Graham crackers- 1 pound

1 Fruitcake, chocolate with nuts, 8 ¼ ounces

2 Packages Filtered Cigarettes- 40 cigarettes[9]

Frau Materne always responded with letters of thanks, as she wrote on December 3, 1967:

Dear Mr. Joseph,

Thank you very much for your lovely package. I am always happy to hear from you. There are not many old friends left from my husband. The circle gets ever smaller.

[. . .] with my small pension, there are no extras, and sometimes I must forgo things. For this reason, coffee and cocoa are always a welcome treat. These things are always very expensive and not affordable on my income.

The workmen like the cigarettes; a good cigarette is more valuable than a tip.

[. . .] Best wishes for your well-being, and in gratitude during the Christmas season,

Martha Materne[10]

Oscar Materne was seventy-six years old when he died, and my father regretted he missed the opportunity to reconnect.

Three or four times a year, every year, Dad sent off the cardboard boxes along with a short note, such as the one he wrote in March 1968: "The little happiness that our packages bring is nothing compared to what we have to thank your husband for. I wish I could do more for you."[11]

The packages continued until 1972. That February, there was a snowstorm, a nor'easter that brought a heavy, wet snow and strong winds to New Jersey. On Sunday morning, February 20, 1972, my father started the day by shoveling the driveway and sidewalk on Vannest Avenue and then driving off to Francis Avenue to take care of the apartments.

As my mother remembered, my father was out for a long time that morning. But then she recalled that he was planning to stop at the drugstore to pick up a bottle of Phillips Milk of Magnesia for her. When the phone call came, my mother heard an unfamiliar voice, a woman who identified herself as a nurse at St. Francis Hospital.

"Your husband has been admitted. You need to come in right away."

"What happened? Is he all right?"

The lady on the other end offered no more information. She only repeated, "You need to come in."

Mom had a hard time reaching me. She called the house phone in the dorm lobby, but I wasn't there. This was the time before cell phones, before you could call or text anyone, wherever they were. The girl who answered offered to take a message.

"No, a message won't do."

I was a senior in college, my last semester before graduation, and Lenny, the boy I had met at the library, had become a serious boyfriend. It was late Sunday morning when a friend knocked on Lenny's apartment door. She wrapped her arms around me before saying words that made no sense.

The roads were still snow-covered and the snowplows were spreading salt on the highway when Lenny and I drove down Route 1 to Trenton, making it impossible to speed. St. Francis Hospital was near the apartments, a familiar structure, at least from the outside.

I felt a tightness in my chest as I stepped off the elevator. There was my mother, sitting on a bench, hunched over, staring at the linoleum floor tiles. Mr. and Mrs. Jacobs had driven my mother to the hospital and stayed until I arrived.

We hugged each other, and all she said was, "It's not good, it's not good."

The cardiologist had explained that my father had suffered an acute myocardial infarction. The next twenty-four hours would be critical.

I entered Dad's room and saw him attached to an IV line, an oxygen tube, and a heart-monitor machine. He was wide awake, but his skin was pale, and when I leaned over to kiss him, I could feel the sweat on his forehead. Dad's speech was clear, and foremost on his mind were instructions on how to find the car. There was a need to deliver this message, and I cried and smiled at the same time, trying to be reassuring.

I stood by the bedside, held my father's hand, and stroked his forehead. His eyes were intensely blue, and he was concentrating so hard to give me the names of streets and directions.

"Please, please, don't worry about the car, just rest, just get better ... I love you, Daddy."

It seemed so unreal. My father was never sick, never in the hospital. On the rare occasions when he spiked a fever, Dad covered himself in a heavy down comforter to "sweat it out."

My father did have occasional leg cramps at night. Massaging the calf muscles relieved the pain, but he didn't consider the episodes serious enough to seek medical attention. He wasn't on any medications, and other than the leg cramps, he never complained of physical ailments.

The doctors limited the time Mom and I could be with Dad to five minutes per hour for one person. I don't know why we didn't question that restriction, but we trusted the medical opinion; we believed rest was what he needed and followed the directive.

I stared at the large clock in the waiting room and prayed Dad could make it past twenty-four hours. Through the afternoon, he drifted in and out of sleep. When I walked into the room, he sometimes said a few words.

My mother and I sat on the bench all day and through the night, praying for a miracle. We squeezed each other's hands, we hugged and cried and alternated brief visits with Dad. I replayed his words about the car.

"Mom, did Dad drive himself to the hospital?"

"That's what they told me."

"But how could he have done that? And he walked himself into the hospital?"

"You know your father."

As the hours of the night slipped into morning, he no longer woke up to the sound of the door opening or the touch of my hand on his head or the sound of my voice.

On Monday morning, February 21, 1972, Dad passed away.

He was 56 years old, not an old man, and there were no signs of an underlying problem that I knew about. Through the night, Dad was still there, and now he was gone. There was a heaviness in the room that kept me from leaving

When Mom and I walked out of the hospital on Monday morning, the sky was a brilliant blue, and the sun was shining on the hard-packed snow. I detested the brightness and cursed the sunshine. It should have been overcast, a dark, gloomy day without sun.

We walked around the corner, followed my father's directions, and found the car, a gold Dodge Coronet, exactly where he said it would be. He had been so proud of his first new car.

I felt numb as I drove slowly on snow-covered roads and fought back tears to stay focused on turns and traffic lights. It hurt to walk back inside our home, to look around at familiar furniture and pictures, and stare out the window. It all looked the same, but everything had changed. We made the necessary phone calls —to Uncle Gerhard, Aunt Miriam, Judi, Barbara and . . . the funeral home.

We buried Dad in the Hebrew Gardens section of Fountain Lawn Memorial Park in Ewing Township. The cemetery is on Eggerts Crossing Road, just a few miles from our house. The gravestones lie flat against the ground, and the sky rests gently on the earth. A small creek flows near the outer edge, and four tall northern white cedar trees stand behind my father's resting spot, like soldiers guarding a sacred place.

After the funeral, friends came to the house to express condolences. Mom told and retold every visitor the events of my father's death. "He was never sick, never. That morning, he had gone out to shovel snow at the apartments, but never came home." The words were a mantra that helped Mom handle the emotions of grief from losing her partner of almost twenty-five years.

The house was filled with people, and words of condolence morphed into social visits, and I hated that. I was twenty-one years old, certainly not a child, but I retreated to my bedroom, not able to engage in conversation with anyone.

For months after my father died, I saw him everywhere. Men walking just ahead of me looked exactly like him, but I never saw their faces, just the back of their heads, the shape and color of their overcoats, or sometimes a quick glimpse of a profile. As I hurried to catch up, they turned a corner and slipped away.

In the weeks following the funeral, I came to the cemetery often, usually once a week, sometimes more, and talked to Dad. I told him about the rejection letters from medical school, which were a disappointment, but not a surprise. My grades and test scores were good, but not outstanding. Rejection was hard to handle. A door had closed on a dream, and I didn't have a clear path forward. But I didn't want Dad to worry about me. Marshalling the optimism and confidence of youth, I reassured him that I would be fine and find another career.

Early in the morning on the last Sunday in June, I spread the old worn yellow blanket on the grass and sat by the graveside. I updated Dad on news of my graduation from Douglass College, and added that I had found a job as laboratory assistant at Rockefeller University in Manhattan.

Most important, I was there to share my wedding day with my father. Four months had gone by since he left me, physically that is. Spiritually, I was still connected. I sat quietly by the gravesite, gently stroking the dirt. He had liked Lenny and would have been happy to know we were getting married. I wanted Dad to have my new address, an apartment in the Bronx, near Albert Einstein College of Medicine, where Lenny would begin medical school, and close to the No. 5 subway line, convenient for me to get to work.

Dad had never met the Grossman family, and I wanted him to know that Lenny's parents, Sam and Pearl, were good people. They had immediately welcomed me into the family, and I was finally getting a brother, Richard, and a sister, Elaine.

Sam and Pearl grew up in New Jersey, and each of their families had lived in America long enough that no one ever thought about the time when a great-grandparent first came over from Europe.

Sam was an army veteran of World War II, as were most of the fathers who lived in Lenny's neighborhood in Saddle Brook. After landing on Utah Beach on the shores of Normandy in August 1944, Sam and the soldiers in the 1306 Engineer General Service Regiment traveled across France building bridges and repairing roadways, often working under attack from exploding German mortar shells. [12]

When the Allies defeated Nazi Germany, the engineers were in southern Germany, in the town of Bamberg, about 40 miles north of Nuremberg. However there was little celebration as the men continued to repair bridges, and rather than hearing about plans to return home, they received orders to deploy to the ongoing war in the Pacific Theater.

Days after Sam and his regiment landed in Manila, the United Stated dropped an atomic bomb on Hiroshima. Three days later, a second atomic bomb destroyed Nagasaki, and on August 15, 1945, Japan surrendered.

The war was now over, but once again, the men had a new assignment: they were being sent to Yokohama as part of the army of occupation in Japan.

As soon as Sam received his orders to return home, he wrote, "You can stop your dreaming Sweets and prepare to live – I will be coming home and very soon." The letter was signed, "I love you. Almost on my way, your Bubi." In December 1945, Sam arrived home.

* * *

Sam and Pearl were so different from my parents. They were committed to community activities, such as the PTA and the school board, and they were part of a strong social network of friends that shared holidays and vacations together.

My father had talked about future trips, about traveling with my mother after I finished college. He had never flown on an airplane, and I wished he had experienced the excitement of being in the clouds, of peering down on earth and seeing the network of roads, bridges, and skyscrapers around Manhattan give way to farms, open spaces and mountains in the West. The resources to travel were there, but the time never came.

I must have been sitting next to my father's grave for almost an hour when I glanced at my watch and realized it was time to leave. My unspoken wish was to have the wedding at the cemetery. I understood the absurdity of this thought, but in a mind of disparate emotions, it made sense.

Finally, I stood up, folded the yellow blanket, said good-bye to Dad and hurried home to get dressed for my wedding.

The ceremony was in a grassy field outside a log cabin, tucked away on the agricultural campus of Rutgers University. It had rained the day before, but on that afternoon, the sun was shining brightly as Lenny and I stood under the chuppah and exchanged our wedding vows.

Evelyn and Ernst, 1957

Ernst and Betty on a Circle Line Boat, 1955

Ernst and Lilo at Niagara Falls

Wedding. Lilo, Evelyn & Lenny, Gerhard, and Miriam
June 25, 1972

9

HONORING THE RESCUERS

"1972—the year of the good and the bad; the year that my husband died and the year my daughter got married. God gave me something good to take away some of the bad."

Mom's words. After my father died, Mom took on tasks she never did before. She paid household bills, handled tenant complaints, and even though she didn't enjoy the role of landlady, found plumbers to fix the leaky pipes and contractors to patch the roof. The apartments continued to be well maintained and fully occupied.

In October, Mom decided to look for a temporary job, "just for the Christmas season." She started in the children's department of Dunham's, a local department store. In a matter of weeks, she got to know the customers who came in often for T-shirts or pajamas or just to stop and say hello to "the nice little lady with a German accent."

Trenton in 1972 had changed from the city I knew as a young girl. As factories closed down and industrial jobs declined, many residents sought employment in the surrounding communities, and families who could afford to, moved to Lawrenceville, Princeton, and across the Delaware River to Yardley, Pennsylvania.

By far the biggest blow to Trenton's economy came from the riots in 1968 following the assassination of Dr. Martin Luther King Jr. During the 1960s, Dr. King was the driving force of the civil rights movement working to achieve racial integration through peaceful demonstrations. He spoke out at a time when "Whites Only" signs were posted above drinking fountains in Birmingham and when George Wallace stood in the doorway and tried to prevent black students from entering the University of Alabama.

In 1968, the country was torn apart by the Vietnam War. Protests against the war began on college campuses, but gained wide spread support as national leaders, including Dr. King, added their voice against a growing number of American lives lost in the jungles of southeast Asia.

The assassination of Dr. King released violence in more than 100 cities across America, including New York City, Baltimore, Chicago and Washington, D.C.

In Trenton, buildings were set ablaze, stores were looted, three hundred people were arrested, and dozens of police officers, firefighters, and residents were injured. Many of the properties set on fire were never rebuilt; lots remained vacant and stores moved out to the suburbs. Hastening the city's decline, the Quaker Bridge Mall, a sparkling two-level regional mall on Route 1, opened in the mid-1970s and siphoned customers away from Trenton.

Dunham's had been a fixture of the Trenton shopping landscape for a hundred years, but the city's economic decline drove the retailer to close its downtown store in 1983, and transfer Mom along with the rest of the employees to a new location, an open-air shopping mall in Lawrenceville.

That was the time of change. Mom sold the apartment buildings and the house on Vannest Avenue. Free from real estate burdens, she downsized to Concordia, an adult community in Monroe Township. Her new place was 10 miles from my home in Plainsboro. At that time, I was a mother with two children, Eric, age seven, and Amy, age four, and Lenny was practicing internal medicine and rheumatology at Rutgers Community Health Plan.

On a chilly October morning in 1985, I watched the moving men load the sofa, piano, chairs, and tables, along with dozens of labeled boxes, into the truck. My mother had lived on Vannest Avenue for twenty-one years. She had moved in as a wife and mother of a teenage daughter. Now a widow, she was moving into a community that would take care of cutting the grass and shoveling the snow.

Mom continued to work at Dunham's, but only part-time. I had started working as a credit analyst for United Jersey Bank, and I needed help with the kids. Mom took Eric and Amy to the movies on school holidays and swimming in the summer and drove them on Tuesday and Thursday afternoons to Hebrew school at The Jewish Center in Princeton.

The Jewish Center, a conservative synagogue, was our religious home. In 1988, when the synagogue planned a program to commemorate the fiftieth anniversary of Kristallnacht, they asked Mom to speak.

People wanted to hear first-hand accounts of life in Nazi Germany. This marked a change from early post-war years when there was little public conversation about the Holocaust. Perhaps emotions were still too raw, but as the war years slipped away, folks were eager to learn more. In 1985, California was the first state to require Holocaust education in public schools and New Jersey followed suit a few years later.[1]

On a cold Wednesday evening in November, Mom recalled the night of broken glass, when she was fifteen years old, the night she looked out her window, saw her synagogue in flames, and heard the screams of people being beaten:

There are many Jews still alive who were in Germany at that time. And when you mention November 9, 1938, they shudder. The Kristallnacht was only the beginning. We should have seen the handwriting on the wall.

Why did my family not leave Germany? There are many reasons. Where should we go? Not many doors were open to us. We never believed that all of us would be killed. We had a very comfortable life in Germany, and the strongest point of all—we were Germans. I can hear my parents say we lived here for generations and my father received the Iron Cross, first class, for bravery during World War I. It will not happen to us my father said. This terrible time will pass.

My mother spoke softly about the deportation of her parents and her brother, and having nowhere to sleep. Her voice lifted as she continued:

A miracle happened! I heard my name called from behind: "Lilo, Lilo, don't run away. Let me talk to you!" This voice came from Eva Cassirer . . . . I worked there as a maid, got a new name, Liselotte Lehmann, and new identification papers.

I just was the lucky one. I was living in hiding with a great Gentile family. It is hard to believe that some people in this time had so much kindness and compassion for Jewish people. They were the real heroes.[2]

The audience of two hundred people sat in silence, taken in by her words. Afterwards, Ruth Fath, a member of the congregation, approached me and said, "Evy, I think I know someone in Princeton who is related to the Cassirers. My friend Isabel is married to Peter Paret, and I believe he and Eva Cassirer are cousins."

I stood astonished and overwhelmed by her words. I nodded, not able to find a response. To me, my mother's history and her survival in Germany were entities from the past, without connection to our current life in Princeton. Yet here was Ruth tying these two worlds together.

Ruth and Isabel, women in their mid-fifties, shared interests as trained psychologists. Beyond their professions, they shared a personal bond, as both had married men born in Germany. Joe Fath, born in Frankfurt, came to the U.S. in 1938, the year of Kristallnacht. He was a past president of the synagogue and an executive in the chemical industry. I knew nothing about Isabel Paret's husband.

Dr. Isabel Paret and Professor Peter Paret welcomed my mother and me into their home on the grounds of the Institute for Advanced Study in Princeton. What I remember most clearly is a large oil painting of a young girl of fair complexion, with shoulder-length brunette hair, sitting on the floor surrounded by playing cards. The girl was Suzanne Cassirer, Professor Paret's mother.

Suzanne's father, Paul Cassirer, and Eva's father were brothers. Paul was a publisher and art dealer, with a gallery in Berlin that exhibited Vincent van Gogh and Paul Cézanne and also promoted the German impressionist Max Liebermann. I believe it was Liebermann who created the painting of the young girl that dominated the living room.

As we entered Isabel and Peter's home, my mother elbowed me and whispered, "He looks so familiar."

Not that surprising, since this Princeton professor was the son of the gentleman who visited Mrs. Sotscheck, the gentleman for whom my mother prepared coffee and cake decades ago, and one of the few people my mother trusted. Mr. Paret had been a regular guest at the house in Berlin ever since he became Eva's financial guardian when her father died.

Professor Paret's journey from his birth in Berlin to the IAS included a few decades in California. Paret, a boy of thirteen, came to San Francisco in 1937 with his mother, sister and stepfather, Siegfried Bernfeld, after his parents divorced. Paret's father, Hans Paret, remained in Berlin.

At nineteen, Paret was drafted and served in the combat intelligence of an infantry battalion in New Guinea and the Philippines during World War II. After the war, he earned a bachelor's degree from the University of California, Berkley, and a PhD from the University of London.

Professor Paret is a scholar, an intellectual who has written numerous books on the intersection of the history of art in the twentieth century with the history of war. But his primary research focused on military history from the 18th to the 20th century, specifically on the Prussian general Carl von Clausewitz.

I sat in their living room in awe of this distinguished scholar, a professor at the IAS since 1986 and before that, at Stanford University and the University of California, Davis. Paret has received numerous awards and has continued to write, publish, and lecture well into retirement.[3]

Professor Paret and Eva are cousins, four years apart in age (Eva is the older one). As children, they knew one another in Berlin and reconnected when Eva came to the United States to study in Los Angeles. He gave me the impression that Eva was very bright, but stubborn and opinionated, and at times, quite demanding. To me, it was fascinating to hear her described by someone other than my mother, who dismissed any flaws or shortcomings.

As we continued our conversation, Paret politely asked my mother about her experience in Berlin and her life after the war. I sensed he knew well the details my mother provided about working as a maid, the Nazis who sat at the dinner table, and the other people in the house that Mrs. Sotscheck and Eva protected.

Ruth Fath had given me an incredible gift. She tied together loose fragments and brought me to the home of an internationally recognized historian who was connected to Eva through both his mother and father.

Ruth came to the synagogue on the fiftieth anniversary of Kristallnacht and heard a woman speak about a family that saved her from deportation. Professor Paret knew that his family protected a Jewish woman during the war, but not who this woman was. Ruth connected the pieces.

* * *

"Mr. Gorbachev, tear down this wall!" President Reagan spoke those words in Berlin as he stood before the Brandenburg Gate. The wall, that stood in the middle of a proud city which had rebuilt itself after World War II, now tore the city apart. Communist East Germany had erected the wall as part of the Cold War struggle between the Soviet Union and the United States. The conflict between communism and democracy played out in Berlin with a wall that separated families for more than twenty years.

On November 9, 1989, two years after President Reagan's provocative words, the wall came down.

Fixed on the TV screen in my living room, I watched men and women pull each other up to stand on top of the wall and use hammers to knock away chunks of the barrier.

I jumped up and down and cheered as families and friends, apart for decades, embraced each other with hugs and tears. But there was one person in particular I wished could have witnessed the reunification of Berlin.

Uncle Gerhard had passed away on June 8, 1989, five months before the wall fell. He was 75 years old and had died suddenly from a massive heart attack. Uncle Gerhard was a brilliant man, an astute reader of history and politics, and a first-hand observer of Germany as it transitioned in the 1930s from a democracy to a totalitarian Nazi state. He would have been overjoyed to witness the wall come down and the reunification of Germany in the following year.

Uncle Gerhard's life had a huge impact on our family, and his experiences in Germany have been passed down to his daughters, Judi and Barbara, and to their children and grandchildren. Judi's grandson, Sam Heimowitz, spoke at his Bar Mitzvah about the tefillin his great-grandfather brought over from Germany, and Barbara's granddaughter, Aliyah Moline-Freeman, paid tribute to the family in a high school essay about true resilience. To Aliyah, her great-grandfather's struggle to come to the United States and her great-grandaunt's survival in Berlin are examples of resilience and stories to be remembered.

Mom carried a box of twelve long-stemmed roses onto the plane at JFK on Monday evening, May 1, 1995. Each flower was tucked into a plastic vial filled with water. The roses were for Eva Cassirer, and they had to be in perfect condition when we arrived in Berlin the next morning.

For years Mom never wanted to go back to Germany, but when an invitation came from the Berlin Senate, Mom accepted with mixed feelings. Germany was trying to make amends for its horrific past, truly an impossible task. The past could not be rewritten or erased, but Germany was facing its shameful history through mandatory classroom education, monuments, museums, and state-sponsored trips, such as the one that was bringing us to Berlin. The program invited those who were persecuted and expelled or those who survived in hiding or in the camps to come for a visit, with expenses paid by Germany.

The trip allowed Mom to see Eva and return to the house that sheltered her. Mrs. Sotscheck had died 20 years ago, and the opportunity to reconnect was gone. But Eva, now a woman in her mid-seventies, was still living in the same house, and we were going back to say thank you.

I sat on the plane repeating, *Ich freue mich so sehr Sie endlich kennen zu lernen* (I'm so glad to finally meet you). My intent was to greet Eva in proper German, and have a bit more to say than just *Hallo, Wie geht es Ihnen?* (Hello, how are you?).

Eva, a petite woman with straight blond hair, was at the airport holding a bouquet of red roses for Mom. The women warmly embraced, exchanged identical flowers, and rapidly began a conversation to fill the gap of almost 50 years. They had exchanged greeting cards and short notes since the war, but never a phone call or photos. There are events you imagine for months, even years, and once they happen, you wish that time would stand still, but all you can do is take a photo.

Eva helped load our luggage into her car and drove us to Café Kranzler, a landmark coffee shop with red-and-white-striped awnings. It had been rebuilt since the war, yet the location and name anchored Mom to memories of childhood. After breakfast, Eva gave us a tour of the city before stopping at the Sophie-Charlotte Oberschule, the school Mom and Eva knew as the Bismarck Lyceum.

I watched Mom and Eva walk around the courtyard, laugh as schoolgirls, and peek into classroom windows and talk about what once was there.

We returned to the car for a 20-minute ride before we pulled into the detached garage on Wildpfad 28. The house was set far back from the street and just as grand as Mom had described. A black wooden front door, over eight feet high, stood recessed in the entranceway. It was positioned asymmetrically between four arched windows, each as tall as the front door. Climbing vines covered the first floor, adding a layer of charm and mystique. Directly above the vines, five large windows filled the length of the second level, and one small window with hinged shutters sat in the center of the dormer on the top floor. Two small chimneys rested on the gently sloped roof and provided visual balance to the stately house.

I stared at the shutters on the bedroom window in the third floor. Those were the ones that Eva had opened when it was safe for Mom to come back inside. The thick grass on the front lawn provided no clues where the grate to the underground bunker once was.

The front door opened into large formal rooms, with shelves filled end-to-end with leather-covered books. The room was unchanged from the time my mother was the maid, but now there were small tears in the brown leather sofa, threadbare patches in the rugs and scratches on the shutters. Yet priceless artwork still filled the rooms. Signed and numbered lithographs by Toulouse-Lautrec hung in the hallway, and a bronze-head statue of Eva by Georg Kolbe sat on top of a shelf filled with journals and stacks of papers.

The kitchen hadn't changed in fifty years: blue cabinets rested against the back wall and black and white tiles covered the kitchen floor. What once was elegant, now was old. Eva showed us the house, even the upstairs bedrooms. Mom picked up photos from the dresser and recalled moments only she and Eva shared, and the two women reminisced, each photo evoking more memories.

I was curious to see the basement and asked if I might take a look. Eva led me down the stairs to a neatly arranged storage area of boxes stacked on top of one another. I had wondered if Mom, Eva, and Frau Riebensahm had hid in a secret underground room when the Russians were stomping overhead searching for women. No, there was no such place, just an ordinary-looking cellar.

With the weather warm, we spent the morning outside on the terrace listening to Eva as she shared bits about her life. After the war, she came to the United States and received a bachelor's degree in astronomy from UCLA in 1952. She continued her studies at the University of London, earning a PhD in philosophy, and then joined the faculty at the University of St. Andrews in Scotland and remained there through the 1970s.

There were a few incomplete personal segments in Eva's narrative, such as a marriage to a Jewish man in New York, which, she quickly added, was short-lived. I would have liked to know more, but I couldn't risk being impolite, so I asked no questions.

After chatting for a while, Mom presented Eva with some gifts. For months, Mom had wrestled with the question of what to buy. Not satisfied with only one gift, we settled on a few: a silk scarf in shades of pink, rose, and mauve, and a Ben Avram lithograph of Jerusalem, the old city surrounded by the gate. On the outside mat, we added words from the Talmud: "Whoever saves one life, saves the whole world."

There was one last gift, a gold bangle bracelet. Eva turned the bracelet round and round, opened the clasp, and read the inscription on the inside: "Thanks for saving my life 1943–1945." The heartfelt words were simple, direct, and true. Eva looked up at Mom and quietly said, "No one has ever given me so nice a gift."

After a night flight from JFK to Berlin and an emotional reunion with Eva, Mom and I were ready to check in to our hotel. However, Eva insisted we join her on a walk with the dogs. How could we refuse? Eva had five Vizslas, sleek, short-haired hunting dogs, all very friendly. Twice a day, every day, Eva exercised her companions with a brisk walk along the trails in Grunewald. She allowed the dogs to run off-lead, and they obediently returned when called. Mom and I managed to keep pace, but we were glad to head back to the Berlin Plaza on Knessebeckstrasse for a much-needed nap.

On Wednesday morning, Eberhard Diepgen, the mayor of Berlin, welcomed our group of about thirty-five visitors to the *Staatsbibliothek*, the city library and said:

We know it was certainly not easy for you to return to a city which for you is associated with such great suffering. . . . We are also aware of the terrible events which had their beginnings here. It is only when we openly face up to our past, when we accept it with all its heights and depths, that we are kept from repeating the mistakes of the past.[4]

Next, a group of young children sang German folksongs. Perhaps it was the sweetness and innocence of their voices, but along with the music, the auditorium was filled with sounds of handbags clicking open and hankies coming out to silence sobs and dry wet eyes.

One of the scheduled activities was a *Dampferfahrt*, a steamboat ride down the Spree River. While the trip offered an opportunity to see sights of the city, it also gave Mom a chance to reconnect with Hans Peter Messerschmidt. Hans Peter, the boy Mom once had a crush on, was still living in Berlin. He had organized a reunion of classmates, and the "boys" were scheduled to meet at Congress Hall. Hans Peter, a tall, white-haired gentleman with a bit of beer belly, held up a sign with Mom's name. He smiled broadly as she stepped off the steamboat and joked that she was still so short.

He had been married four times. He and his current wife, who was Israeli, lived on the outskirts of Berlin, and they invited us to their home, but Mom declined. There were many other places to visit and time was short.

One of those places was Hektorstrasse 19. The Jacoby family had lived on the top floor, and the four-story apartment building where Mom grew up was still in good condition. We were curious to see what it looked like inside but too timid to knock. Before leaving, Mom pressed her face against the front door windows but couldn't see anything through the dark tinted glass.

The next stop was Linienstrasse 5. My father's house had been destroyed in the war, and I was curious to see if another building was now there. Still nothing, just an empty lot.

On the way back to the hotel, we stopped at a fish restaurant and ordered the traditional *weisser Spargel* (white asparagus) with hollandaise sauce. I asked Mom how she felt to be back in Berlin.

"Everything has changed. I don't feel like I'm coming back home. I feel like a visitor."

The Berlin Mom once loved as a young girl, a city with dance classes, swimming pools, wonderful bakeries, and a home with her parents and brother were all gone. Yet Mom wanted to connect to this modern city teeming with traffic and construction projects. To distance herself completely would diminish the memories she treasured and deny what once was there.

We talked about meeting Hans Peter and his decision to remain in Berlin. Now, nearly fifty years later, Mom had no regrets over leaving Germany.

* * *

Each place, except for one, triggered mixed emotions. The most difficult site to see was a memorial sculpture on Grosse Hamburger Strasse, near the deportation center. *Jüdische Opfer des Faschismus (Jewish Victims of Fascism)*, created by Will Lammert, is a haunting piece of thirteen bronze figures, emaciated men, women, and children. The figures stand tall, straight, and angular, and their heads are held up high. There is no emotion in their faces as they stare off into a void, into a place of unspeakable evil. A monument stands next to the sculpture with the inscription:

This was the location of the first Jewish Old Age Home in Berlin.

In 1942, the Gestapo changed that to a Headquarters for Jewish people.

55,000 Berliners of all ages, infants to the elderly, were sent to the concentration camps, Auschwitz and Theresienstadt, and killed in a bestial manner.

NEVER FORGET
BEWARE OF WAR
GUARD THE PEACE [5]

There were flowers in front of the monument and stones on top, for this monument is a tombstone. Mom remembered the day she and her brother waited across the street and saw their parents for the last time. Hans was holding a note that was impossible to deliver. The letter of apology from Anna Marie had arrived too late.

Here, at the memorial stone, the bitter memories came crashing back. There was no escape from the truth of what happened to those who came here.

Just a block away from this painful spot stands a beautiful synagogue. The gold-latticed dome of the New Synagogue on Oranienburger Strasse towers over the neighborhood and creates a powerful symbol of Jewish presence in Berlin. This magnificent dome, designed in the Moorish style with oriental motifs on the façade, has been part of the Berlin skyline for more than 150 years.

On May 7, 1995, the eve of V-E Day, the 50th anniversary of the end of WWII, our visiting group had been invited to the rededication of the New Synagogue. The synagogue had been badly damaged by Allied bombs, but was now largely restored.

More than 2,000 people gathered in the open area behind the synagogue for the ceremony. Tight security was in place with sharpshooters positioned on rooftops of the surrounding buildings. Dozens of media reporters and cameramen were there to cover the event.

We heard Jerzy Kanal, head of the main Jewish organization in Berlin, say, "Today, with this rededication, we are looking especially to the future. We want to fill this building with Jewish life."[6]

It was a miracle that this synagogue was not destroyed on Kristallnacht. On that night, a German policeman, Lieutenant Otto Bellgardt, dispersed a Nazi mob and prevented them from setting the synagogue on fire.[7] To honor this German officer, a group of 22 Jewish policemen from New York City were there that evening.

As the rededication ceremony progressed, it started to rain. Umbrellas went up, ladies covered their hair with plastic bonnets, and people abandoned their seats to stay dry inside. Mom and I stayed outside, moved closer to the front, just a few rows behind Chancellor Helmut Kohl.

I thought about the celebrations in London and Paris to commemorate the Allied victory, and I wondered how the everyday German, the man in the street, was reacting to Germany's defeat. I posed the question to a young man sitting next to me: "Is the anniversary of the war's end, of Germany's defeat, difficult for Germans? What does Germany have to celebrate?"

I expected a nuanced reply. I thought he would express ambiguous emotions such as, "It's complicated," or "Personally, I never harbored any ill feelings towards Jews."

He was far too young to have served in the war, but I wondered what he might know from his father or grandfather. He looked directly at me and said, "The war brought death to hundreds of thousands of Germans—fathers, husbands, and sons. The end of the war brought peace and liberation."

In this crowd it was easy to believe that antisemitism no longer existed. Yet the next day, the newspapers reported that arsonists had set fire to a synagogue in Lubeck, vandals had toppled more than 100 tombstones in a cemetery outside Berlin, in a section reserved for victims of the Nazis, and the police had detained seven young people at a rock concert in Potsdam where they chanted "Sieg Heil" and sang Nazi war songs.

* * *

The day before we were scheduled to leave Germany, we spent the afternoon with Eva and her friend Claus-Ullrich Simon, an art historian. We had moved beyond our conversations about the past, which had consumed us on the first day. Now we were able to consider topics of current interest, especially those we found fascinating. Simon told us about a Polish artist, Stefan Norblin, whose murals he had come upon while traveling in India. Intrigued with the artwork, in which Norblin had joined the color and style of art deco with traditional Indian motifs, Simon began working on a book about Norblin, a forgotten artist, who had spent the war years decorating palaces of the maharajas.

Eva spoke about her years in Scotland, teaching at the University of St. Andrews, and her conversations with various poets. She read aloud her poems about meeting the poet laureate of Scotland, a brilliant alcoholic who fascinated her.

For me, the story of my parents' survival in Nazi Germany had captivated me for decades. Coming to Berlin gave me the opportunity to explore streets with names I'd heard since childhood and walk through rooms of a villa that had protected my mother. Most of all, the trip had allowed me to meet Eva and say thank you.

The Eva I met was a fascinating person—an intelligent, strong-willed woman who had defied the Nazis when she brought my mother into her home.

That evening, Eva invited us out for dinner at an Italian restaurant. I regret that I no longer remember the name of the restaurant, but I know we toasted each other with a glass or two of wine. At the end of the meal, Eva gave us gifts, beautiful plates from KPM, the Royal Porcelain Factory in Berlin, and a special present for Mom.

My mother unwrapped the small box and smiled as she recognized a bracelet and earrings that Eva once wore. The jewelry pieces were crafted with gold and turquoise beads, a present Mrs. Sotscheck had given her daughter many years ago.

We walked out of the restaurant in high spirits. Mom and Eva linked arms, sang old songs, and danced down the street. With misty eyes they embraced and said farewell.

* * *

The trip to Berlin allowed me to thank Eva, but an obligation remained. I needed to have Mrs. Sotscheck and Eva recognized as Righteous Among the Nations. That is the honorary title Israel bestows to non-Jews who risked their lives to save Jews during the Holocaust. That did not happen for a while; I was derailed by a focus on work and family, and the moments in Berlin slipped into the background.

Thursday, September 16, 1999, Lenny and I were returning home from Chicago with an empty car. We had unloaded suitcases for Amy into her freshman dorm, and settled Eric, a senior, into his apartment. Both kids were enrolled at the University of Chicago. Saying good-bye was tough, much harder for me than for them. But I took comfort knowing they were in the same city and the same school, even if it was 800 miles away from home.

We had stopped at midday for lunch and early in the evening for gas and a snack before getting back on the Pennsylvania Turnpike. It was windy and drizzling, with forecasts of heavy rain as Hurricane Floyd was moving up the East Coast. We decided to continue driving and reach home before the storm hit.

It was my turn to drive, and a few minutes after we got back into the Jeep Cherokee, the truck in front of me crossed into the left lane. A sizable tree had fallen onto the highway, with its branches obstructing most of the right lane. I turned the steering wheel to the left and immediately felt the car lurch out of control. We skidded, hit the median barrier, and came to a stop. The Jeep was perpendicular to the fast lane of traffic, in a perfect position to be hit. Lenny unfastened his seat belt and jumped out to direct oncoming traffic. A few cars drove by, heeded his signals, and stayed in the right lane. In the distance, I saw the headlights of a truck coming closer and not slowing down. Lenny ran back to the Jeep, got in, and closed the door, but without time to fasten his seat belt.

There was a loud crash, the sound of screeching brakes, tires skidding, and a low, guttural scream I had never heard before. My husband had somehow been thrown from the car and was lying on the pavement underneath the trailer, perhaps twenty feet away. He was yelling for help, screaming that he was going into shock.

I was shaken by the impact, but not badly hurt. I tried to get out of the car, but the driver's side was pinned against the center median of the turnpike and the passenger side was jammed against the cab of the tractor-trailer. I searched the floor mats for the cell phone to call an ambulance. All I found was broken glass.

Very soon I heard the sirens. The emergency medical technicians lifted me out and brought me to Hershey Medical Center. With a few stitches, an ER physician closed the lacerations in the back of my head. Lenny had already been brought by helicopter to the hospital. They assured me he was being taken care of, but when I asked, "Will he be able to walk?" no one answered that question.

The next day, Spence Reid, the orthopedic surgeon, came into my hospital room. He explained that my husband had suffered numerous fractures in both legs and ankles. Dr. Reid's gentle demeanor and slow and careful speech were immediate clues of the seriousness of the injuries.

The tractor had hit the passenger side at an angle that released the door open, and the force of the impact ejected Lenny. The tires of the truck's cab ran over his legs, broke bones, ripped skin and tissue, and tore off the heel pad from the left foot. Dr. Reid had spent ten hours in the operating room piecing together his shattered bones and re-attaching the heel.

The right femur had suffered multiple compound fractures, but Dr. Reid was optimistic about recovery of that leg. However, the degloving injury below the left thigh down to the foot and uncertainty over the viability of the left heel pad created a far more serious situation. Dr. Reid wanted to consider amputation.

I was stunned and scared, but for the moment, I needed to see my husband.

Having lost my glasses in the crash, I stumbled down the hallway and pressed my face to the number on each door until I found his room.

Lenny was attached to a ventilator, and there was an external fixator on his right leg, and another on the left supporting the foot and ankle. The left foot was raised up and held in position by a pulley and weight. External fixators, metal rods attached to the bone by pins and screws, look like medieval torture devices.

I sat by his bed and wept. I thanked God for saving my husband's life, and I prayed that he would walk again. I stroked his hand and then looked at his face. It was perfect—not a scratch, not a bruise, not a mark. Nothing. As terrible as the impact was to his lower body, his face and arms were untouched. Thank you, dear God, thank you.

The whole family made their way to Hershey—Lenny's parents, Pearl and Sam; his sister, Elaine; his brother and sister-in-law, Richie and Phyllis; their boys, Aaron and Harold; my mother; and Eric and Amy. I had just hugged my kids good-bye yesterday. That seemed like a long time ago.

By Sunday morning, Lenny was off the ventilator. As we entered the room, he looked at all of us standing there and said, "So, the whole mishpacha's here."

Just hearing him talk brought us a sigh of relief. The family went home on Sunday afternoon, and Amy broke down in sobs when it was time to leave. Reluctantly she returned to college, but Eric refused, and I couldn't persuade him otherwise.

Eric and I spent the next three and a half weeks at a nearby motel. We fell into a pattern of being in the hospital early in the morning when the surgeons made rounds. We paced around the hospital during the operations—surgeries to exchange the external fixators with internal rods and plates, and skin grafts to replace torn skin with healthy tissue.

Ten days after the accident, the surgeons brought my husband into the operating room for debridement and possible amputation. In debridement, the wounds are cleaned and any infected or dead tissue surgically removed. The question of amputation was still unresolved. Dr. Reid and his team planned to probe the heel pad, examine the foot, and make the final decision in the operating room.

Lenny understood the possible outcome of this surgery. He had discussed the options with his team of surgeons and had already thought about the shape of the stump and a future life with a prosthesis.

Two hours into the operation, the phone rang in the family waiting area. Sam, Pearl, Mom, Eric, and I were sitting there in silence. I picked up the phone, and heard Dr. Reid say, "Good news, the heel pad is bleeding. We're not doing the amputation."

On the night of the accident, Dr. Reid had re-attached the heel, but he was not at all certain if the blood vessels would reconnect. Now he knew. With a viable heel, the foot could be saved. I looked at my family and conveyed the good news with a thumbs-up and a smile that required no words.

There was one other factor that closed the case against amputation. The skin below the knee was not strong. It would need to be grafted, and that would not serve well as a durable stump cover. In Dr. Reid's opinion, the best course of action was to keep the foot and the leg.

Hallelujah! Hallelujah!

For me, that was the most emotional day since the accident. There were still a few more scheduled procedures, but the major question was answered.

When we left Hershey Medical Center after twenty-six days, Lenny had undergone six operations and had lost twenty pounds.

He was transferred to Princeton Hospital, where the nurses and staff knew him as Dr. Grossman, the physician who came in daily to make rounds on his patients. Over the next month, Lenny underwent three more surgeries for debridement of wounds and grafts to the left foot, plus many hours of physical therapy. All along, countless friends and colleagues brought food and flowers and heartfelt wishes for a complete recovery.

In mid-November Lenny came home to a house transformed to meet his needs. A long wooden ramp stretched over the front steps and allowed me to push the wheelchair through the door. The furniture on the first-floor was rearranged to allow for a hospital bed in the middle of the living room.

After four weeks at home, confined to bed and unable to bear weight, Lenny was admitted to St. Lawrence Rehabilitation Center to begin the next phase of recovery.

The physical therapists at the rehab wasted no time. With the help of parallel bars for support, they brought him to a standing position, and for the first time in weeks, he saw the world from six feet tall. The days in St. Lawrence were focused on exercises to strengthen muscles, improve mobility in the knees, and test the ability of the reconstructed left foot to bear weight.

* * *

How do you adapt when faced with a life changing accident? How do you live in a country when the leader pursues the "Final

172

Solution?" And how you do adjust to a new country with new traditions?

For my parents, grit and determination along with that necessary ingredient of luck brought them to shelter in the heart of Berlin. And wanting to be part of American life, my mother tried new recipes, such fruit-filled Jello molds and relied on Chef Boyardee for authentic American spaghetti and meatballs.

For my husband, a strict and rigorous exercise schedule helped restore his strength. When Lenny returned home from the rehab center, he pushed himself with daily workouts—squats, walking up and down the stairs, and pedaling the indoor bike.

The injuries in Lenny's legs are permanent, and there is chronic pain. The reconstructed heel on his left foot needs to be wrapped daily with gauze bandage rolls and protected with padded socks, and even then, there are times when the skin breaks and bleeds.

Years ago, Lenny completed three marathons. The last one was in New York City in 1995 when he and Eric ran together, each of them encouraging the other to the finish line. That is no longer possible. Instead, Lenny has become a strong long-distance cyclist, able to cover 50 miles or more on a weekend ride.

I have watched my husband and my parents deal with pain by pushing it away. My parents have shielded me by hiding terrible memories, yet there are times when that's impossible.

Each year the Rutgers Jewish Film Festival hosts a number of international movies with a wide range of Jewish content. Last year my mother and I saw *The Mover,* a Latvian film based on the true story of Zanis Lipke and his family, who saved Jews from the killing fields of Riga by hiding them in a bunker underneath his house. Tears poured down my mother's face as she sat in the theater watching men, women and children march to their death in a field in Riga, the same place where her parents were murdered.

This memoir is primarily a story of my parents' survival during the Holocaust, but the accident in September 1999 is an integral part of our family story, a story that called upon strength and adaptation when everything we accepted as ordinary suddenly changed.

* * *

A few days after Labor Day in 2009, when the weather still belonged to the hot, humid days of summer, Mom and I boarded the train at the Princeton Junction railroad station for a meeting in Manhattan. Mom was 86 but if you didn't know her age, you'd easily believe she was ten years younger. She had retired only five years ago from the job she originally took in 1972, "just for the Christmas season."

Dr. Mordecai Paldiel welcomed us into his office at the International Raoul Wallenberg Foundation (IRWF), an organization which researches Holocaust rescuers and promotes educational programs worldwide.

Wallenberg, a Swedish diplomat, saved tens of thousands of Hungarian Jews by issuing papers identifying the holders as Swedish citizens and housing them in buildings protected by diplomatic immunity. In January 1945, Wallenberg was arrested by the Soviets and taken to Moscow. More than ten years elapsed before the Soviets issued a statement that Wallenberg died of a heart attack in 1947, yet rumors remain that he was tortured and executed while in prison.

The impact of Wallenberg's life has been recognized in numerous countries, including memorial parks in Budapest and Stockholm, monuments in New York City, Israel and London, and the efforts of the IRWF.

Mom and I had come to the IRWF to meet Paldiel, who had been the director of Yad Vashem's Department of the Righteous for over 20 years. In that position, he had read more than a thousand Holocaust rescue narratives and had written a half dozen books about rescuers from more than 40 countries. These men and women came from varied backgrounds such as farmers, businessmen, housewives, Catholic nuns, and Protestant minister, yet they all shared a common code of morality and a willingness to save another at the risk to their own lives.

To nominate someone as Righteous Among the Nations, Yad Vashem required a signed testimony with a detailed account of the rescue and an independent document to authenticate the event.

Paldiel listened as my mother told her story. He asked a few questions, reviewed the documents we brought along that morning, and forwarded the paperwork to Yad Vashem. Along with my mother's testimony, Professor Paret agreed to submit a narrative from information he independently knew.

The response from Yad Vashem arrived a year later. When I opened the envelope, I was overjoyed to read of the organization's decision: "We are pleased to announce that the Commission for Designation of the Righteous has decided to award the title of 'Righteous Among the Nations' to Hannah Sotscheck and her daughter, Eva Cassirer."

However, that happiness was muted by Eva's passing. Eva had died on September 19, 2009, less than a month after my mother and I had submitted our application to Yad Vashem. She was 89 years old, and my efforts to give her the title she rightly deserved were initiated too late.

On a Thursday evening in May 2012, Lenny, Mom, and I walked into the Bronfman Center for Jewish Life on the NYU campus in Manhattan. The Israeli Consulate office in New York had organized an award ceremony in which a medal and certificate of honor would be presented to the Righteous or their heirs.

I had asked Professor Paret to accept the award, but initially he refused. "I did nothing to deserve this," he said. "If anyone should accept it, it should be your mother."

In time, Paret had a change of heart. I believe he agreed as a favor to Mom.

In addition to Eva and Mrs. Sotscheck, four groups of rescuers were being honored that evening. They included a woman from Lithuania who saved a six-year-old girl who crawled out from under the barbed wire of the ghetto, a Danish couple who hid a young Jewish boy, and two sets of rescuers from the Ukraine, a gentleman who smuggled food into the ghetto for a woman and her daughter and a family who hid two brothers in their henhouse for 14 months.[8]

Wearing a crimson jacket with a black-and-white striped jersey, Mom walked up to the stage, stood on her tiptoes to see above the podium, and shared her story. Paret followed and spoke warmly about his cousin, Eva. The Israeli consul presented the awards to Paret, and never wanting to accept them, days after the ceremony he mailed the medal and certificate to my mother.

Dr. Paldiel had come to celebrate with us and had prepared a bulletin board with photos of Mrs. Sotscheck, Eva and Mom. Uncle Gerhard's granddaughter, Cynthia Davis, and her husband, Howard Lev, were there, along with a handful of our friends.[9]

Towards the back of the auditorium, Isabel Paret and Ruth Fath sat next to each other. Twenty-four years ago, Ruth had come to hear Mom speak about broken glass and synagogues on fire, and she heard the name Cassirer. Ruth was the person who made this evening possible, the person who completed many pieces of an unfinished jigsaw puzzle, and the connector who brought Princeton and Berlin together.

* * *

I had not forgotten about Paul and Leni Pissarius, the couple who sheltered my father and grandparents. The problem was that I had no one to authenticate my father's account of the time he spent in hiding.

Searching randomly on the internet, I stumbled on an article, "*Die Eisenbahnstrasse*," (The Railroad Street), by Waltraud Schwab in the *Kreuzberger Chronik* (*Kreuzberg Chronicle*), published in December 2005. The opening lines grabbed my attention:

My Railroad Street belongs to Paul Pissarius, the old neighbor from the back house of number 15. Many times, he has told how at night, during the blackout, he and the boy walked the short distance from his house to Köpenicker Strasse. They had the dead man on a cart. He tells how they had to cross the street with the corpse when everything was dark. They had fear. It was endless. It was sitting in their knees and in their throats. Every noise was a danger. A match, they could not light.

Not even when they threw the dead man into the River Spree, on the Brommy Bridge. The boy had to help. The dead man was his father.[10]

They threw the dead man into the river . . . The boy had to help . . . the dead man was his father. I read the words over and over and over. Stunned and frozen, I stared at those words. *Eisenbahnstrasse. Paul Pissarius.* Here was my father's story, my father's secret. Who was this Waltraud Schwab and how dare he expose my family secret?

The article continued. Pissarius and his wife lived in a small ground-floor apartment in the back house of Eisenbahnstrasse 15. They hid three Jews, a man and wife and their son, in a tiny room for two and a half years. All the pieces fit together. It was painful to read. How did Waltraud Schwab know all these details?

Slowly, I came out of my fog of disbelief and realized I had to contact Schwab. It was August of 2009, when I first emailed him.

I am writing to you about your article, "Die Eisenbahnstrasse." The three people in hiding were my father and grandparents. What my father needed to do when my grandfather died was a story my family knew, but never discussed.

Waltraud Schwab turned out to be a she, and her first reaction was: "So, it was true."

With that initial introduction, we began exchanging emails. Schwab had moved into the fourth-floor apartment on Eisenbahnstrasse as a student in 1978 and lived there for almost twenty years, except for time in London from 1986 to 1989. When she first met Pissarius, he was 83, and his wife, Leni, had died the previous year. The neighbors regarded Pissarius as an eccentric old man, and didn't believe his crazy story of saving three Jews. No one believed him. Even Schwab had doubts. She described Pissarius as follows:

A thin man with alert eyes and big ears . . . Pissarius was old when I first met him. That, I then thought, was the reason why almost every time I met him, he told me that he had hidden three Jewish people for two and a half years. . . .

Today, I however think, Pissarius told this story over and over again, because it was the most important event in his life. He had done something that complied with his humanitarian convictions. I am sure I asked him, why he helped—but I can't really remember his answer. It then seemed to me, that his wife was the driving force. From what I remember, he very often said: "My wife said, we do this. My wife said, our house won't be bombed."[11]

When a block of houses across the street, adjacent to DeTeWe, a telecommunications factory, was completely demolished by Allied bombs, the back house on Eisenbahnstrasse 15 only suffered damages to an outside wall. Leni was right.

Schwab described Pissarius as a lonely old man, disappointed by the lack of recognition from the German government and the silence from the people he had rescued. He could not remember their names and did not know what had happened to them after they left Germany.

The unexpected connection to me brought Schwab to search the State Archives in Berlin, where she found a file with a photo of Leni and Paul (the only photo I have) and a few documents. One was an application to the Compensation Office dated October 5, 1964. In it, Leni explained how she and her husband sheltered my father and grandparents during the war. She wrote that her husband received a small monthly pension, but she had no income.

Along with Leni's application, there was a document written by my father:

I can confirm that the information provided by Mr. and Mrs. Pissarius is true. It is correct that they gave us shelter from January 30, 1943 to the end of the war. For 27 months, they carried this tremendous risk. It was a great deed, the significance of it cannot be overstated. I am pleased to read that the city of Berlin intends to honor these fellow citizens. Please let me know when the ceremony will take place. If it is possible, I would like to come to Berlin and be there for this opportunity.[12]

Leni's efforts succeeded, and the German government provided her a small monthly pension. However, the pension ended when Leni died. There was no ceremony and my father never went to Berlin.

* * *

Werner Pissarius sat comfortably on a wicker chair at the Ratscafé in Andernach, a picturesque town on the Rhine. It was Monday afternoon, December 12, 2011, a cloudy day that hinted of rain.

The old gentleman with thinning blond hair and twinkling blue eyes was sporting a patterned silk burgundy cravat with a white shirt and jacket. He was dressed up for a special occasion. He had large ears, just like his uncle Paul.

A few months earlier, I had received another letter from Yad Vashem, this time stating that Paul and Leni would be awarded the title of "Righteous Among the Nations." It was wonderful to read those words, but then the letter requested a name and address of their nearest relative, someone to accept the award.

I had no name to send them.

Somewhere a daughter and a grandson existed. That much I knew from Schwab's emails, but nothing more.

Finding a relative was a challenge that required more resources. I emailed Dr. Paldiel. He suggested I contact Beate Kosmala, the director of the Silent Heroes Memorial Center (*Gedenkstätte Stille Helden*).

Until that time I knew nothing about the memorial center. Later, I had the opportunity to visit this small museum tucked away on a side street in the center of Berlin. It is focused on the people who protected Jews during the Nazi dictatorship. They are the "silent heroes." Using tables with touch screen computers, the museum weaves together stories of Jews who went into hiding along with the actions of their rescuers. This little-known museum is a gem.

Taking Paldiel's advice, I emailed Dr. Kosmala. Two days later, she replied:

I can hardly believe it, but today I found a relative of Paul Pissarius, his nephew, Werner! But, can you imagine, he is 96 years old. During the phone call, he told me the whole story! He knows of a grandson, Peter, but unfortunately doesn't remember his last name. Peter was the son of Paul Pissarius' daughter. I don't give up finding the grandson, but I give you now the nephew's address.

We never found the daughter or the grandson, but I was thrilled that we located Werner, and that he was happy to accept the award given posthumously to his aunt and uncle.

That is what brought Lenny, Mom, and me to the Hotel Rheinkrone in Andernach. Our hotel was next to the historic Rheintor, a medieval gate that immediately conjures up images of knights in armor. The hotel faced the Rhine, and we walked a short way along the river before heading up a cobblestone path to the Ratscafé.

The café was filled with Werner's friends and family, and a few reporters, all seated around tables covered in red-and-white checkered tablecloths. Towards the back, a woman with wavy auburn hair and wire-rimmed glasses sat alone with a notebook on her lap. Waltraud Schwab, the neighbor and journalist, had traveled from Berlin to be with us.

Emmanuel Nahshon, the chargé d'affaires of the Israeli Embassy, had flown in from Berlin that morning. He greeted us warmly and began the ceremony by introducing Werner and inviting him to speak. With a strong voice, Werner began:

My name is Werner Pissarius. I was born in 1915 in Eberswalde. I was and am the nephew of Paul and Helene Pissarius, who now post-mortem will receive the title Righteous Among the Nations. In the following words, I will try to tell you why my uncle and aunt received this high honor. This is possible, since I had close contact with my uncle since childhood. Until I was six years old, I lived with my grandparents, also the parents of Uncle Paul. I was, so to say, the younger brother by 20 years. After the Second World War, Uncle Paul and Aunt Leni often came to visit, and we talked about the event that stayed in their heart and became memorable to me.[13]

I listened to Werner retell the story of my grandfather's death, my family secret, the story memorable to both of us.

When Werner finished speaking, I stood by my chair and pulled out a few sheets of paper. I watched him nod and smile as I spoke in German to offer my deepest gratitude. Prepared for this moment by college classes and online lessons with a teacher who became my friend, Dietlinde Alphart, I stood up in the Ratscafé and said:

Mein Name ist Evelyn Joseph Grossman, und ich bin die Tochter von Ernst und Elisabeth Joseph. Ich freue mich so sehr, hier mit Ihnen zu sein und Ihnen, Herrn Pissarius meine tiefste Dankbarkeit zu bezeugen.

My name is Evelyn Joseph Grossman, and I am the daughter of Ernst and Elisabeth Joseph. I am very happy to be here and convey my deepest gratitude to you, Mr. Pissarius.[14]

I went on to speak about my father's decision to meet Paul and Leni, despite his uncertainty and fear. That was certainly the best decision he ever made.

I shared the story of my mother's survival, my parents' emigration and the start of a new chapter in their lives.

The ceremony continued with a few more speeches followed by final words from Nahshon:

In the sea of darkness where the Jews of Germany and Europe perished, there were a few points of light. Little stars in the darkness of the empty sky. Strong people that followed their conscience and not the orders of their leaders. . . .

There were a few. Too few. They could only save a handful of lives, a small number compared to the millions who were murdered. They could not change the course of history, but their courage will always remain in our memory. The "Righteous among the Nations," to whom Paul and Helene Pissarius belong, are the brightest stars in the sky of humanity.

As a Jew and a representative of the State of Israel, I am very proud to honor their memory here today.[15]

I stood tall behind Werner as Nahshon presented him the medal, and I smiled broadly as the two men held up the certificate of honor for the photographers.

That day Werner accepted an award for his uncle and aunt, however he was also a man of compassion and humanity. In the 1980s, Werner and his wife, Gretel, helped three young boys, triplets, in Burkina Faso, a poor, small, landlocked country in West Africa. For more than twenty years, Werner sent packages of food, clothing, and toys, including soccer balls and bicycles, to Lassané, Adama and Ousseini Ouédraogo.[16]

Along with the presents, Werner wrote countless letters, always encouraging the boys in their school work, and sharing their joy when each graduated high school and went on to study at the university.

Indeed, Werner and Paul Pissarius had far more in common than sparkling blue eyes, thinning hair, and large ears.

The day after the ceremony, Lenny, Mom, and I boarded the train for the six-hour ride to Berlin. After a night's rest at the Hotel Orion in Charlottenburg, the district where my mother grew up, we explored the neighborhood and found Santas on every corner, waving nonstop, and sidewalk trees wrapped with holiday lights.

Late in the afternoon a cab driver brought us to the Kreuzberg district. Small apartment houses stood close together. Graffiti covered the doors, and kids rode bikes in the street. The cab stopped at Eisenbahnstrasse 15 where Waltraud Schwab was waiting for us.

We went behind the apartment house facing the street and into the courtyard where the *Hinterhaus*, the back building, stood. Schwab pointed to the top floor, where she had once lived, alongside neighbors who dismissed the stories Pissarius told.

On the side of the building, a dusty, faded, pale yellow and pink curtain covered a cracked ground-floor window. That was the window of the room where my father and grandparents had hid. I stood there silently for a long time, trying to penetrate the cloth, the dirt, the dust, and the years.

The hours of daylight are short in December, and twilight was rapidly fading into darkness as our little entourage entered the building. We walked single-file down a dull green, dimly lit narrow hallway. I rang the doorbell. No answer. I rang the bell again and this time a young woman cautiously opened the door. I spoke haltingly in German and explained why we were there. She looked solemnly at me and nodded but said nothing. I wasn't sure she understood. A child was playing in the background and the fragrant sent of cumin floated through the air. The young woman politely smiled and closed the door. I was disappointed that I couldn't enter, but I reminded myself that a young family lived there today. The room that sheltered my father and grandparents existed in the past and in my imagination.

As the three of us walked away, I thought of Dad walking in the hallway, opening the door, and stepping out into the courtyard. I stopped for a final look at the window. There were three stories above the ground-floor apartment, and I wondered about the other tenants in the building. Had they not noticed a man leaving the building early in the morning and coming back with packages? Had they questioned who he was? Or had they chosen to keep the secret?

Waltraud Schwab came along with us as we walked silently down to the river, retracing the funeral steps from long ago. It was cold night that night as I stood by a metal fence on the dock. Off a few feet stood the foundation of the old Brommy Bridge, all that remained from the bridge destroyed during the war.

I came as close as possible to the past.

* * *

Back at home, I found an old shoebox with photos, papers, and my father's notes:

These 27 months of my life I will never forget. And I shall never forget this time for a special reason. I live today because I was saved by people who risked their lives to help my family and me . . . in spite of all the hatred and in spite of all the atrocities against the Jewish people, there were Germans who did not agree with what was done to the Jewish people. They did not criticize openly. They did not fight against the Nazis, but they helped their Jewish friends to survive. They gave shelter to hide these people from the Gestapo, the first and most important step for survival. Others supplied food. By doing these acts of humanity, they risked everything they had including their lives and the lives of their families. What these few Germans did was so great, that their deeds should be reported and not forgotten.[17]

I grew up in a peaceful time and can only try to understand the evil of the past through conversations, notes, and documents. My dad has been gone now for more than 45 years, but his words remain in my heart, and he will always be a part of me.

My parents have given me a treasure chest of stories to remember and pass on to future generations.

This July, Mom will celebrate her 95th birthday. She lives independently, in the same house where she's been for more than 30 years. She is in good health, physically and mentally, but uses a cane to steady her balance. The person my mother was during the war years is the same person she is today. She is full of energy, enjoys connecting to people, chatting with neighbors, and sharing a bit of gossip. And people respond kindly to her.

To mark this milestone birthday, we're seeing *My Fair Lady* on Broadway. When the final curtain falls, I imagine Mom will carefully pick up her cane, sing a few notes of her favorite songs, and gracefully dance out of the theatre, wondering how we will celebrate next year.

Reunion of Eva Cassirer and Lilo, May 1995

Reunion in Berlin: May 1995: Lilo, Evelyn and Eva

May 2012, New York, Righteous Among the Nations
Ceremony honoring Hannah Sotscheck and Eva
Cassirer. L to R: Israeli Consul Gil Lainer, Lilo, Professor
Peter Paret and German Consul Elmar Jakobs

December 12, 2011, Andernach, Germany: Righteous Among the Nations Ceremony honoring Paul and Helene Pissarius. Front L to R: Werner Pissarius, Lilo; Rear L to R, Minister of the Israeli Embassy, Emmanuel Nahshon, Evelyn & Lenny, and Sandra Witte, Press Secretary of the Israeli Embassy in Germany.

Werner Pissarius holding the Certificate and Medal of Honor. Behind him, L to R: Martina Fuchs, Werner's adopted daughter, and Evelyn

Berlin, 2011, L to R: Waltraud Schwab, Evelyn, Lilo

Lilo's 90th Birthday. Front row L to R: Josephine and
Knox (Eric's children) and Evelyn. Back row L to R: Amy,
Lenny, Elizabeth (Eric's wife) and Eric

April 2015, Evelyn, Lilo, and Amy

November 2017, Lilo and great-grandson, James

AFTERWORD

This is a book that I struggled to write, but had to complete. From childhood, I've known the outline of my parents' story, but the details required decades of conversation, travel, research, writing, and editing. Conceiving of the book as a multi-generational memoir, I've added my perspective, drawing especially from my personal experience in the post-war years as well as my connections to relatives of the rescuers.

There is an additional story, a painful event, that cannot be omitted. My daughter, Amy, died on March 16, 2017. She was 36 years old. It is now more than three years since Amy passed away.

It happened suddenly, on a day of bright sunshine and blue skies following a snowstorm that had covered central New Jersey. That Thursday afternoon, Amy walked out of her apartment to clean off her car. While brushing away the snow, she suffered a cardiac arrest and fell to the snow, still holding the ice scraper in her hand. The paramedics came, but Amy had already slipped away.

The loss of my daughter left a void in our lives that can never be filled. Amy was an artist. As a young girl, she loved drawing, painting, and playing the piano. She would spend hours with crayons and markers, and those pictures morphed into large oil compositions with patterns of color, primarily shades of brown, olive green, and splashes of yellow and burgundy. In one of her earliest works, a boy is playing a cello. The neck of the cello runs through the boy's shoulder forming a single unit, as though the two were meant to be together. Many a time I have stood in the living room, directly in front of the painting, and stared at the calmness and serenity in the boy's face and gently ran my fingertips across the canvas.

Amy was an art teacher and taught in various schools, first in Fort Worth and later in Philadelphia. She would tell me about the projects she assigned, such as drawing sneakers and dragons, and how the kids would stop by the art room after school to chat and spend a few minutes finishing their work. Her students loved her.

Through Amy I learned to see beauty in ordinary objects. I watched her create jewelry from broken earrings, circuit breakers, metal faucet washers, and covered electrical wires. She fashioned a bracelet for me from buttons of various size and color. It is spunky and unique and pure Amy.

Amy struggled with medical problems, some that we knew about and others that remained hidden. In her early thirties, she noticed a hearing loss that was later diagnosed as the result of bilateral acoustic neuromas. Proton therapy, radiation treatment focused on the tumors in her brain, prevented total hearing loss, but the damage was significant. Amy also struggled with mental illness. She battled depression with medication, exercise, and sessions with therapists. Sometimes it helped.

Amy died suddenly, without warning, and her passing has left me broken in spirit. I loved Amy deeply, and I still do. Death does not take that away. But I can no longer hug her or hear her laugh. I miss her terribly. Holidays and birthdays are reliable triggers of grief, but unexpected events such as the scent of perfume or background music in the supermarket can also evoke sharp and bitter pain.

Lenny and I visit the cemetery every Sunday afternoon. We stand together and share memories, silence, and tears. Amy lies next to my dad in the Fountain Lawn Memorial Park, and it gives me comfort to know he is protecting her in the world to come, just as he always protected me.

My mother often asks why she is still alive and Amy is gone. That question has no answer. Throughout her life, my mother has dealt with the pain of grief, and Amy's passing added another layer of sorrow. Her death ran counter to the expected order of the young outliving the old. Time and age gave my mother familiarity with death, but experience provided no solace with the loss of a granddaughter.

I talk about Amy all the time; that gives me comfort. Friends are sometimes reluctant to mention my daughter, afraid they will cause additional pain. Nothing can be further from the truth. I love talking about Amy. I love remembering her, even when my voice breaks, and I dig deep in my pockets for a tissue to wipe away the tears.

Mom and I spend hours together looking at old photos and sharing memories, and in our grief, we support each other. We remember trips to graduation ceremonies in Chicago, a city Amy and Eric adored. After receiving their undergraduate degrees, they both stayed in Chicago to continue their education. Amy earned a master's degree in art history from the University of Illinois at Chicago, and Eric went on to study medicine at the University of Chicago, where he fell in love with Elizabeth Myers.

Eric and his wife Elizabeth are now the proud parents of three beautiful children, Josie, Knox, and James. Elizabeth, a dermatologist, cares for patients in her Santa Barbara office, and Eric, a pediatric surgeon, operates on children ranging in age from newborns to teenagers.

Josie, Knox, and James are still young, and while they love seeing their great-grandma, Grandma Lilo, they don't yet know her story of survival in Germany. That will come, but for now, I'm quite happy to watch them play in the yard and jump on the trampoline.

ACKNOWLEDGMENTS

Traveling to Berlin, walking the streets where my parents grew up, and seeing the Stolpersteine, the stumbling blocks placed in front of buildings to remember those who once lived there, made me promise to write my parents' story.

Writing this book has been a journey, and I have many people to thank for their help along the way. I owe the greatest thanks to my mother, who shared her memories and answered my endless questions with honesty, humor, and love. As this book goes to publication, my mother is now 97 years old, and thankfully, she remains in good health.

My father passed away many years ago, yet I remain deeply grateful for his love and protection and his notes and old letters, all of which I've tried to honor in this book.

To understand my parents' past, I needed to put together a jigsaw puzzle, but some of the pieces were missing. Many were destroyed or lost, but some were found by luck, such as the article written by Waltraud Schwab, a gifted journalist. Thank you, Waltraud, for believing in Paul Pissarius and helping me understand a man I never met, but wished I had.

Thank you to Ruth Fath, who came to The Jewish Center in Princeton on the fiftieth anniversary of Kristallnacht. Were it not for Ruth, I would never have met the professor who lived just a few miles away and knew the story of how his family protected a young Jewish woman during the war.

With deep sadness, I must add that Professor Peter Paret died on September 11, 2020. I am thankful for his friendship and his testament of tribute for the two women who saved my mother's life.

Researching and writing this story called for me to learn German, at least to a level where I could engage in simple dialogue and read old letters. Thank you to my German teacher, Dietlinde Alphart, for helping me conjugate irregular verbs and for countless hours online in conversation and friendship.

Along with preserving my parents' story, I wanted both sets of rescuers to receive the recognition they deserved. Thank you to Mordecai Paldiel, who helped me navigate the requirements of Yad Vashem and who celebrated with us when Eva Cassirer and her mother were honored as Righteous Among the Nations.

Many pieces of this jigsaw puzzle came together from the notes of my father's brother, Uncle Gerhard. I am thankful for his description of coming to America and for the many conversations with my cousins. Thank you to Judi and Barbara for information about family relations and remembering our grandmother's favorite perfume, Eau de Cologne 4711.

After I finished my first draft of the manuscript, I joined a writing group at the Hamilton Library, led by Rodney Richards.

Thank you to Rod and all the fellow writers who listened as I read and gave me immediate feedback on what worked and what needed revisions. At that time, I also started working with Anne Horowitz, a wonderful editor, who offered valuable insight and encouraged me to include my voice, as well as my parents', in telling their story.

The final steps of this journey came together through the dedication of Dr. Liesbeth Heenk and Amsterdam Publishers. Thank you, Dr. Heenk, for helping me move rapidly through the publishing process and transforming my words into a published book.

My daughter Amy was very close to her grandma. Amy encouraged me to preserve Grandma's story, and I wish she were here to see the book in print. Yet I believe that Amy and my father are cheering me on, happy to know the writing is finally completed.

More than anyone else, I am grateful to Lenny, my best friend and my husband, who carefully read every draft and supported me through this long journey with encouragement, humor, and love.

NOTES

2. Seeking Shelter

1. Documents from the International Tracing Service. Ernst Joseph/Lippmann was compulsorily employed by Siemens-Schukertwerke AG, Berlin, from April 8, 1941 to February 1943.
2. Gerhard Joseph, written notes. My cousin, Judi Davis, gave me a copy of her father's notes that provides an understanding of his academic work in the University of Berlin, the antisemitism he encountered, and the challenges he faced in emigrating to the U.S. and finding a sponsor.
3. Gerhard Joseph, written notes.
4. Gerhard Joseph, written notes.
5. Ernst Joseph, written notes, July 1963. My father left me notes describing how he came into contact with Paul and Leni Pissarius and some of his experiences living in hiding.
6. Beate Meyer, Hermann Simon and Chana Schütz, *Jews in Nazi Berlin, From Kristallnacht to Liberation* (Chicago, University of Chicago Press, 2009) p. 90.
7. Holocaust Education & Archive Research Team, "Berlin, The City and the Holocaust."http://www.holocaustresearchproject.org/nazioccupation/berlin.html
8. United States Holocaust Memorial Museum, "German Jewish Refugees, 1933–1939" Holocaust Encyclopedia, https://www.ushmm.org/wlc/en/article.php?ModuleId=10005468

3. Eisenbahnstrasse

1. Werner Pissarius, "Personal Reflection on Paul and Helene Pissarius", Yad Vashem Commemoration, Andernach, Germany, December 12, 2011.
2. Ernst Joseph, written notes, "When I was young," July 1963.

4. The Jacoby Family

1. Cammin was a rural county in the government district of Stettin, the former province of Pomerania.
2. United States Holocaust Memorial Museum http://www.ushmm.org/wlc/en/article.php?ModuleId=10007901 http://fcit.usf.edu/holocaust/TIMELINE/TEXTLINE.HTM

3. http://www.owlnet.rice.edu/~rar4619/nuremburg.htmlhttp://www.jewishvirtuallibrary.org/jsource/Holocaust/nurlaws.html

4. https://www.huffingtonpost.com/rabbi-evan-moffic/joachim-prinz-march-on-washington-speech_b_3814893.html "The Forgotten Speech at the March on Washington, 8/26/2013

5. Elisabeth Joseph, speech written and presented at The Jewish Center, Princeton, New Jersey, fiftieth anniversary of Kristallnacht, November 1988.

6. Shoah Research Center, Berlin, The International School for Holocaust Studies www.yadvashem.org/odot_icrosoft%20Word%20-%205995.pdf

5. Alone

1. Transport I/1 from Berlin, Germany to Theresienstadt, Ghetto, Czechoslovakia on 02/06/1942, The International Institute for Holocaust Research. http://db.yadvashem.org/deportation/transportDetails.html?language=en&itemId=5092960

2. Mathilde Bing, letter written at Grosse Hamburger Strasse detention center, "Collection Camps – the First Stage of Deportation." On June 28, 1943, Mathilde Bing was taken to Auschwitz and murdered. Wolfgang Benz, Barbara Distel, *Der Ort des Terrors: Geschichte des nationalsozialistischen Konzentrationslager,* Volume 9 (C.H. Beck, 2005), p. 47.

3. Lodz, United States Holocaust Memorial Museum. http://www.ushmm.org/wlc/en/article.php?ModuleId=10005071

4. Berlin, United States Holocaust Memorial Museum. http://www.ushmm.org/wlc/en/article.php?ModuleId=10005450

5. The Eichmann Trial, Yad Vashem, The World Holocaust Remembrance Center. http://www.yadvashem.org/holocaust/eichmann-trial

6. Erica Fisher, *Aimée and Jaguar: A Love Story, Berlin, 1943,* translated from the German by Edna McCown (Los Angeles: Alyson Publications, 1995). Felice's friend, Inge Wolf, worked as a housekeeper for Elisabeth Wust, a gentile mother of four boys and the wife of a Nazi officer. Through Inge, Felice and Elisabeth became friends and their relationship evolved into a deep and dedicated love. When my mother and Felice met, Felice (known as Jaguar) had not yet moved in with Elisabeth (known as Aimée). In 1999, this book by Erica Fisher was made into a German drama film, *Aimée & Jaguar.*

7. Peter Wyden, *Stella* (New York: Simon & Schuster, 1992), pp. 152-153.

6. Hiding

1. Jim Falk, "Cassirer and Cohen-draft family genealogy," metastudies.net http://metastudies.net/genealogy/ZDocs/Stories/storiesN2_1c.html

2. Elisabeth Joseph, "Living with Mrs. Sotscheck," notes from conversation on March 3, 2002.

3. Roger Moorhouse, "Berlin At War," (New York, 2010), pp. 285-291.

4. The Bombing of Civilians in World War II, *World Future Fund.* http://www.worldfuturefund.org/wffmaster/Reading/war.crimes/World.war.2/Bombing.htm

5. Es war das Haus der Habanera - Berlin - Tagesspiegel Wikipedia contributors, "Notable residents in Grunewald," *Wikipedia: The Free Encyclopedia*, https://en.wikipedia.org/wiki/Grunewald

6. Elisabeth Joseph, "Life after the War," notes from conversation on April 2, 2003. A similar event was documented in the film, "Die Unsichtbaren-Wir wollen leben." The Invisibles-We Want to Live. An article on the Yad Vashem site documents the number of Jewish soldiers in the Russian Army and the U.S. Armed Forces, "Jewish Soldiers in the Allied Armies", Yad Vashem, http://www.yadvashem.org/holocaust/about/combat-resistance/jewish-soldiers

7. Ruth Gay, "Safe Among the Germans, Liberated Jews after World War II," (New Haven and London, 2002), p. 147.

8. Moorhouse, op. cit., p. 306; Gay, op. cit. pp. 146-147.

7. The War Is Over

1. Hans Peter Messerschmidt. Oral testimony, File # 13856, *USC Shoah Foundation Institute*, Interview date, April 24, 1996 http://collections.ushmm.org/search/catalog/vha13856 In his testimony, Hans Peter stated that in January 1945 he was taken out of Auschwitz, forced to march to Gleiwitz, and then transported to Buchenwald. Buchenwald was liberated by the U.S. on April 11, 1945. Peter was very weak when Buchenwald was liberated, and he did not return to Berlin until August 1945.

2. Yad Vashem contributors, "Transport 19, Train Da 403 from Berlin, Germany to Riga, Latvia on September 9, 1942," *The International Institute for Holocaust Research* http://db.yadvashem.org/deportation/transportDetails.html?language=en&itemId=5092665

3. Yad Vashem contributors, "Transport 30 from Berlin to Auschwitz Birkenau, Extermination Camp, Poland on 26/02/1943," *The International Institute for Holocaust Research* http://db.yadvashem.org/deportation/transportDetails.html?language=en&itemId=5092739

4. International Tracing Service, Document ID#s: 507219, 507266, 507376.

5. Danuta Czech, *Auschwitz Chronicle: 1939-1945*, (New York: Henry Holt and Co., 1990), 55, 57 and Auschwitz-Birkenau Memorial Museum contributors, "IG Farben" and "The Beginning of Construction," http://auschwitz.org/en/history/auschwitz-iii/ig-farben After the war, twenty-four members of IG Farben's board of directors were indicted by the U.S. military tribunal. The

trials took place in Nuremburg and lasted from August 1947 to July 1948. Thirteen men were found guilty of "war crimes against humanity." Otto Ambros, Managing Director and Production Chief for Buna Rubber, was a prime perpetrator of the atrocities. He tested poisons and chemicals on concentration inmates, and he oversaw the Buna Rubber plant in Auschwitz. Ambros was sentenced to an eight-year prison term. The injustice of this lenient sentence was further amplified by his early release in 1952. Four years in prison was an insult to the families of the thousands who died in the factory at Monowitz.

6. International Tracing Service, Document ID# 507219, treated in the infirmary from September 14, 1943 to September 23, 1943, Document ID # 507266, treated in the infirmary from October 26, 1943 to November 4, 1943 and Document ID # 507376, treated in the infirmary from December 27, 1943 to January 1, 1944.

7. Judi Davis genealogy research. Erika's mother, Auguste Brill, and Ernst's mother, Betty were sisters. Auguste and her husband, Bernhard Zimche, were deported and murdered at Auschwitz. Erika survived through her marriage to an Aryan, Bernhard Krause.

8. "Social Democracy for the 21st Century: A Realist Alternative to the Modern Left," http://socialdemocracy21stcentury.blogspot.com/2013/07/us-unemployment-in-1930s.html and Gerhard's notes.

9. Richard Breitman and Allan J. Lichtman, *FDR and the Jews* (Cambridge: The Belknap Press of Harvard University Press, 2013), Quote from Democratic representative Martin Dies of Texas, 105.

10. Jon Blackwell, "1934: The Top Cop is King of Rackets," *Trentonian,*www.capitalcentury.com/1934.html and Jon Blackwell, "1926: Wet and Wild Prohibition Days," *The Trentonian* www. capitalcentury.com/1926.html

11. Gerhard Joseph notes.

8. Life in America

1. Ann S. Petluck, Director Migration Services, report on Ernst and Elizabeth Joseph, December 28, 1948.

2. Ibid.

3. Autobiography of Erich Jacobs: and this is my life story, by Erich Jacobs, Leo Baeck Institute.

4. Ernst Joseph, notes July 1963.

5. Barbara Freeman. "Re: Family History." E-mail to Evelyn Grossman, July 17, 2017. Judi Davis. "Re: Family History." E-mail to Evelyn Grossman, July 22, 2017.

6. Oscar Materne, letter to Ernst Joseph, December 10, 1962.

7. Ernst Joseph, letter to Oscar Materne, November 18, 1964.

8. Martha Materne, letter to Ernst Joseph, January 14, 1965.

9. Ernst Joseph, letter to Martha Materne, March 5, 1968.

10. Martha Materne, letter to Ernst Joseph, December 3, 1967.

11. Ernst Joseph, letter to Martha Materne, March 5, 1968.

12. Max Schwartz, *Bridges to Victory, Story of the 1306 Engineers in WWII* (Max Schwartz/Consulting Engineers, Inc. 2003); Executive Committee 1306 Engineers' Historical Society, *The History of the 1306th Engineer General Service Regiment.*

9. Honoring the Rescuers

1. Lawmakers from 20 states pledge to mandate Holocaust education ... https://www.jta.org/.../united-states/lawmakers-from-20-states-pledge-to-mandate-holo...In California, Holocaust education was required in the public schools for grades 7 through 12. In NJ, Holocaust education was required for all students in the public schools.

2. Elisabeth Joseph, speech given at The Jewish Center, Princeton, NJ, November 9, 1998; Barbara Preston, "Kristallnacht vigil hears Survivor tell of Night of Horror", *The Princeton Packet*, November 11, 1988.

3. Peter Paret died on September 11, 2020. He was a Fellow of the American Academy of Arts and Sciences, a Member of the American Philosophical Society, which awarded him its Thomas Jefferson Medal. He was also an Honorary Fellow of the London School of Economics and an Honorary Member of the German Clausewitz Society, which in 2020 awarded him its Silver Pin of Honor. The Federal Republic of Germany had honored him with the Order of Merit Cross, First Class in 2000 and Great Cross in 2013.

4. Eberhard Diepgen, Mayor of Berlin, Welcoming Address, May 3, 1995.

5. www.elephantinberlin.com/2012/12/first-jewish-cemetery-groe-hamburger.html

6. Alan Cowell, "German Paradox: Alongside Healing, New Flames," *New York Times International*, May 8, 1995; https://www.nytimes.com/1995/05/08/world/berlin-journal-german-paradox-alongside-healing-new-flames.html

7. There are many reports crediting police officer Wilhelm Krützfeld for protecting the New Synagogue on Kristallnacht. However, it was Lieutenant Otto Bellgardt, the officer of the local police precinct who dispersed a Nazi mob; Senior Lieutenant Wilhelm Krützfeld, head of the local precinct later covered up for him. Pompeo visits Berlin synagogue desecrated during Kristallnacht, http://www.israelnationalnews.com/News/News.aspx/271340.

8. In addition to Hannah Sotscheck and Eva Cassirer, the other people honored were: Brone Budreikaite, Lithuania, Gerard Van Raan and Gerda Van Raan-Lubach, the Netherlands, Mikhail, Maria and Vasili Gunchak, Ukraine, and Aleksey Varvaretsky, Ukraine

9. Dan and Elizabeth Zibman, Sally Steinberg-Brent and Marsha Stickler came to the ceremony.

10. Waltraud Schwab, "Die Eisenbahnstraße," Kreuzberger Chronik, December 2005 / January 2006. http://www.kreuzberger-chronik.de/chroniken/2005/dezember/strasse.html

11. Waltraud Schwab email, September 12, 2009.

12. Ernst Joseph, letter to the Compensation Office in Berlin. February 9, 1965.

13. Werner Pissarius, Speech at the ceremony in Andernach, Germany, December 12, 2011.

14. Evelyn Grossman. Speech at the ceremony in Andernach, Germany, December 12, 2011.

15. Emmanuel Nahshon, Greetings at the ceremony in Andernach, Germany from the Israeli Embassy, December 12, 2011.

16. Lassané, Adama and Ousseini Ouédraogo, "Drei zum Leben," (Wagner Verlag, 2012); This book was written by the triplets in memory of the Pissarius Family and Elisabeth Kugler, a development aid worker who first met the boys when they were infants. The book includes stories about growing up in Burkina Faso and many photos of the boys as young children and photos of the boys as young adults when they traveled to Andernach to meet Gretel and Werner Pissarius.

17. Ernst Joseph, notes, summer 1963.

BIBLIOGRAPHY

Berkovits, Annette Libeskind. *In the Unlikeliest of Places: How Nachman Libeskind Survived the Nazis, Gulags, and Soviet Communism.* Canada: Wilfrid Laurier Press, 2014.

Breitman, Richard and Allan J. Lichtman. *FDR and the Jews.* Cambridge: The Belknap Press of Harvard University Press, 2013.

Czech, Danuta. *Auschwitz Chronicle: 1939-1945.* New York: Henry Holt and Co., 1990.

Fisher, Erica. *Aimée and Jaguar: A Love Story, Berlin, 1943.* Translated from the German by Edna McCown. Los Angeles: Alyson Publications, 1995.

Gay, Ruth. *Safe Among the Germans, Liberated Jews after World War I.* New Haven and London: Yale University Press, 2002.

Goldsmith, Martin. *The Inextinguishable Symphony: A True Story of Music and Love in Nazi Germany.* New York: John Wiley & Sons, Inc. 2000.

Gossman, Eva. *Good Beyond Evil: Ordinary People in Extraordinary Times*. London and Portland: Vallentine Mitchell, 2002.

Gross, Leonard. *The Last Jews in Berlin*. New York: Simon and Schuster, 1982.

Levi, Primo. *Survival in Auschwitz*. Translated from the Italian, *Se questo è un uomo*. New York: Touchstone, Simon and Schuster, 1996.

Meyer, Beate, Hermann Simon, and Chana Schütz, eds. *Jews in Nazi Berlin, From Kristallnacht to Liberation*. Chicago: University of Chicago Press, 2009.

Moorhouse, Roger. *Berlin at War*. New York: Basic Books, 2010.

Ouédrago, Lassané, Adama Ouédrago, and Ousseini Ouédrago. *Drei zum Leben*. Wagner Verlag, 2012.

Schwartz, Max. *Bridges to Victory, Story of the 1306 Engineers in WWII*. Los Angeles: Max Schwartz/Consulting Engineers, Inc. 2003.

Schwartz, Mimi. *Good Neighbors, Bad Times: Echoes of My Father's German Village*. Lincoln and London: University of Nebraska Press, 2008.

Wyden, Peter. *Stella*. New York: Simon & Schuster, 1992.

ABOUT THE AUTHOR

Evelyn Joseph Grossman was raised in Trenton, New Jersey, by parents who wanted to embrace American culture yet couldn't separate themselves from their German past and German accents. She earned a bachelor's degree from Douglass College, Rutgers University, and a master's degree from Fordham University. In her professional life, she worked as a financial analyst in the field of commercial debt obligations. In retirement, she has focused on writing her parents' story, honoring the rescuers as Righteous Among the Nations, doing volunteer work in social service programs in Trenton, going on bike rides with her husband, Lenny, and taking trips to California to visit her grandkids.

HOLOCAUST SURVIVOR TRUE STORIES

The Series **Holocaust Survivor True Stories WWII**, by Amsterdam Publishers, consists of the following biographies:

1. Among the Reeds. The true story of how a family survived the Holocaust, by Tammy Bottner

Amazon Link: getbook.at/ATRBottner

2. A Holocaust Memoir of Love & Resilience. Mama's Survival from Lithuania to America, by Ettie Zilber

Amazon Link: getbook.at/Zilber

3. Living among the Dead. My Grandmother's Holocaust Survival Story of Love and Strength, by Adena Bernstein Astrowsky

Amazon Link: mybook.to/ManiaL

4. Heart Songs - A Holocaust Memoir, by Barbara Gilford

Amazon Link: getbook.at/HeartSongs

5. Shoes of the Shoah. The Tomorrow of Yesterday, by Dorothy Pierce

Amazon Link: getbook.at/shoah

6. Hidden in Berlin. A Holocaust Memoir, by Evelyn Joseph Grossman

Amazon Link: getbook.at/HiddenBL

7. Separated Together. The Incredible True WWII Story of Soulmates Stranded an Ocean Apart, by Kenneth P. Price, Ph.D.

HOLOCAUST SURVIVOR MEMOIRS

The Series **Holocaust Survivor Memoirs World War II** , by Amsterdam Publishers, consists of the following autobiographies of survivors:

1. Outcry - Holocaust Memoirs, by Manny Steinberg

Amazon Link: getbook.at/Outcry

2. Hank Brodt Holocaust Memoirs. A Candle and a Promise, by Deborah Donnelly

Amazon Link: getbook.at/Brodt

3. The Dead Years. Holocaust Memoirs, by Joseph Schupack

Amazon Link: getbook.at/Schupack

4. Rescued from the Ashes. The Diary of Leokadia Schmidt, Survivor of the Warsaw Ghetto, by Leokadia Schmidt

Amazon Link: getbook.at/Leokadia

5. My Lvov. Holocaust Memoir of a twelve-year-old Girl, by Janina Hescheles

Amazon Link: getbook.at/Lvov

6. Remembering Ravensbrück. From Holocaust to Healing, by Natalie Hess

Amazon Link: getbook.at/Ravensbruck

7. Wolf. A Story of Hate, by Zeev Scheinwald with Ella Scheinwald

Amazon Link: getbook.at/wolf

8. Save my Children. An Astonishing Tale of Survival and its Unlikely Hero, by Leon Kleiner with Edwin Stepp

Amazon Link: getbook.at/LeonKleiner

9. Holocaust Memoirs of a Bergen-Belsen Survivor & Classmate of Anne Frank, by Nanette Blitz Konig

Amazon Link: getbook.at/BlitzKonig

10. Defiant German - Defiant Jew. A Holocaust Memoir from inside the Third Reich, by Walter Leopold with Les Leopold

Amazon Link: getbook.at/leopold

CPSIA information can be obtained
at www.ICGtesting.com
Printed in the USA
LVHW082003041220
672994LV00022B/586/J

9 789493 231108